AN OPEN HEART

The Mystic Path
of Loving People

Yitzhak Buxbaum

Volume Two
THE JEWISH SPIRIT BOOKLET SERIES

THE JEWISH SPIRIT BOOKLET SERIES
Yitzhak Buxbaum, Editor

THE JEWISH SPIRIT BOOKLET SERIES on Jewish spirituality will answer such questions as: "How can I be a Jew in a meaningful way?" and "How can I be a Jew so that it affects my life deeply?" The booklets will attempt to provide a gateway to a deeper and more fulfilling involvement in Judaism for both beginners and committed Jews by offering elevated ideals and practical help to those seeking to make real spiritual progress.

The booklet format has been chosen so that essential and exciting teachings on Jewish spirituality and mysticism can be made available in an accessible and affordable way to the largest audience. The goal is to further Jewish renewal by reuniting the Jewish people with the rich spiritual treasures of Judaism.

Topics in Jewish spirituality will be treated in a way to interest people Jewishly learned and those well advanced on the spiritual path, but also to interest and be fully accessible to Jews who are non-scholars and to those just beginning their Jewish quest.

JEWISH SPIRIT booklets will try to make Jewish spirituality truly popular. They will be be inspiring, concise, informative, and useful. They will be authored by people of different religious tendencies, who represent a broad spectrum of those working to renew Jewish spirituality.

Titles in THE JEWISH SPIRIT BOOKLET SERIES:

Vol.1 Real Davvening
Vol.2 An Open Heart

Some forthcoming titles:

How to Develop Faith and Trust in God
The Essentials of Jewish Meditation
Jewish Mysticism in a Nutshell
An Introduction to Traditional Jewish Mantras

We welcome submissions for inclusion in the series. Please send manuscripts or proposals to THE JEWISH SPIRIT BOOKLET SERIES (see address on p.96).

Library of Congress Cataloging-in-Publication Data
Buxbaum, Yitzhak
An Open Heart: The Mystic Path of Loving People / Yitzhak Buxbaum
ISBN 0-9657112-2-6
1. Mysticism - Judaism 2. Spiritual life - Judaism
LCCN 97-093470

CONTENTS

Dedication; Acknowledgments   6

Introduction: Mysticism and Humanism   7

  Mystic Goals   9

    LOVE FOR GOD, D'VEKUT   9

    LOVE FOR HUMANITY AND AN OPEN HEART   10

  The Mystic Path   10

  Expanding Circles of Love   11

The History of Jewish Mystic Humanism   13

  The Torah   13

    AN IMAGE OF GOD   13

    THE FOUNDERS OF JUDAISM   15

      Abraham

      Moses

  The Teachings of the Ancient Rabbis   17

    ABOUT ABRAHAM'S HUMANISM   17

    ABOUT MOSES'S HUMANISM   18

    LOVE AND THE GOLDEN RULE: HILLEL AND RABBI AKIBA   19

    HUMANITY IN GOD'S IMAGE AND MYSTICALLY ONE:
      RABBI AKIBA AND BEN AZZAI   20

    CLEAVING TO GOD BY IMITATING HIS LOVING ATTRIBUTES   21

    THE STORY OF THE TWO BROTHERS   22

  The Kabbalah: Rabbi Moshe Cordovero's
  Palm Tree of Deborah   24

  Hasidism: Rabbi Israel Baal Shem Tov   25

    A MYSTIC LOVE FOR FELLOW JEWS   25

    THE BAAL SHEM TOV'S SPIRITUAL LEVELS   26

    OTHER EXAMPLES OF THE BAAL SHEM TOV'S
    LOVE FOR PEOPLE   27

Love Him More

How Could I Wait?

The Musar Movement:
Rabbi Noson Tzvi Finkel of Slobodka   29

Essential Teachings of Mystic Humanism   35

Mystic Love of Neighbor as Your Own Self   35

Love of Your Neighbor *is* Love of God   36

Love for Essence, Love for Virtue   37

Attaining Mystic Love   38

MYSTIC VISION: LOOKING AT A PERSON'S SOUL   39

A Loving Person   40

Lessons in Mystic Love   41

ANGER AND PATIENCE   42

NOT JUDGING OTHERS AND FORGIVING
THEM THEIR FAULTS   42

LOVING ENEMIES AND THE WICKED   43

IDENTIFYING WITH OTHERS' SUFFERING   48

D'vekut of *Ratzo* and *D'vekut* of *Shov*   49

THE BESHT'S BABY GRASPS HIS FATHER'S BEARD   53

RABBI SHNEUR ZALMAN'S LESSON TO
HIS SON ABOUT A BABY   54

RABBI SHNEUR ZALMAN LEAVES HIS PRAYING
TO HELP A WOMAN   54

MORE IMPORTANT THAN ECSTASY   56

D'vekut with All of Creation
but Especially with People   57

Understanding the *D'vekut* of
Imitating God's Love   59

PERSPECTIVES FOR UNDERSTANDING   60

Mystic Motives in Loving and
Serving Fellow Humans   64

Mysticism and Love   66

Practical Lessons   69

Learning to See the Divine Image   69

Learning to Imitate God's Love   71

Family   72

Work   73

Good Deeds and Volunteer Work   73

    FIXING THE BED   74

Striving to Achieve   77

Conclusion   79

Notes   82

Glossary   88

A NOTE TO THE READER

Although the language in this booklet refers to God as King, Father, He, and Him, God is not corporeal, has no gender, and is not a male. Men and women are made in God's image (Genesis 1:27), and God has both masculine and feminine traits.

A Note about Rabbis Mentioned in the Text:
Rabbis are often identified by the context as to their period or movement affiliation. Otherwise, rabbis not specifically identified may be assumed to be hasidic, except for the following: Rabbis Yohanan, Tanhum, Meir, and Joseph were ancient rabbis. Rabbis Joseph Kimhi and Eliezer Papo were Sephardic. Rabbis Meir'l of Tiktin, Isaiah Horowitz, the Hafetz Hayim and the Kelmer Maggid were non-hasidic. Rabbi Abraham Isaac Kook was non-hasidic, with hasidic leanings.

Dedication

This booklet is dedicated to the blessed memory of my holy master, the great *tzaddik* and the hasid of his generation, Rabbi Shlomo Carlebach. Shlomo was a model for loving all people, without exceptions. He loved Jews, regardless of their Jewish observance, and all non-Jews too. Shlomo looked at the inside, the soul, not at the outside. It is one thing to talk about loving people and not judging them, it is another thing to live that way. Shlomo was a true mystic and lover of humanity. My holy Rebbe. May God open my heart to love people as Shlomo did.

Acknowledgments

I would like to gratefully acknowledge the help of friends who read the manuscript of this work and offered valuable suggestions to improve its composition and clarity: Justin Lewis, Jane Enkin, Cecelia Urban, Fran DeLott, Sonia Kovitz, Rabbi Simcha Weinberg, and Mindy Ribner. I am grateful also to Rabbi Meir Fund who was always ready to provide information or advice when needed about any Jewish topic.

INTRODUCTION
MYSTICISM AND HUMANISM

Many Jews who seek to deepen their Jewish spirituality
have developed an interest in mysticism. What is the relation
between mysticism and religion? Mysticism means passing
beyond belief and observance to direct spiritual experience.
A Jewish mystic tries to attain *d'vekut*, God-consciousness, a
devotional awareness of God's presence. God is everywhere,
say the mystics, there is no place where He is not present. If
we do not see the Divine Presence, it is only because our eyes
and hearts are not directed to God.

Jews today are also attached to humanism, the Jewish ideal
of loving and serving (helping, doing good to) other people.
Both Hillel and Rabbi Akiba were asked to state the essence
of the Torah. Rabbi Akiba's answer was "love your neighbor
as yourself." Hillel's answer was the Golden Rule – what is
hateful to you, do not do to your neighbor – which is the rule
for the application of the commandment to love. Humanism
is the core Jewish teaching that puts humanity and being
loving and humane at the heart of religion. Although it is
often said, truly, that Judaism gave monotheism to the world,
it is equally true and important that Judaism gave humanism
to the world. In ancient times, people did not understand
religion as necessarily connected to morality. Judaism, the
Torah, taught the world that God is one and humanity is one,
that people are precious to God, and that loving and being
good to them is the essence of serving God.

Both mysticism and humanism are important branches of

Judaism. But what is the connection between them? If one searches in the Kabbalah or in hasidic mysticism, humanism does not seem to have the prominent place that one would expect from the statements of Hillel and Rabbi Akiba that love of neighbor is the essence of the Torah. In the Kabbalah, one learns much about heavenly matters – about the ten *sefirot* (divine emanations) and the four worlds – but less about loving people. Some kabbalists developed an ethical system, but ethics are not at the heart of their mystic perspective.[1] Hasidism brought kabbalistic mysticism from heaven down to earth and concentrated more on earthly matters and on people. Rabbi Israel Baal Shem Tov, the founder of Hasidism, and some of the hasidic rebbes who followed him were great lovers of humanity. But, although Hasidism has many examples of noble humanistic teachings, Jewish humanism still does not appear at the core of the philosophy of hasidic mysticism. Moreover, hasidic mysticism usually focuses on love for fellow Jews and neglects love for non-Jews.

Because, like many others, I am strongly interested in both Jewish mysticism and Jewish humanism, I have searched through traditional sources to find the connection between them. I also wanted to find the connection between these two parts of my own soul. I discovered hidden treasures of wisdom in the tradition. Using insights and clues from many texts, I have attempted to more fully integrate Jewish humanism into the Jewish mystic perspective. This view, which I call Mystic Humanism, means trying to develop the mystic vision to see the holiness of fellow human beings and putting love and service of people at the center of one's mystic path and lifestyle.

One reason to emphasize religious humanism is that there is a constant tendency for people to forget its importance. It is often easier to study Torah, pray, and celebrate Sabbaths and holidays, than it is to truly, religiously love and serve

other people, even those closest to us. Therefore, there is
a need today to reestablish – even within the boundaries
of Jewish mysticism – the centrality of humanism to the
worship of God.

There is another need of the hour too. Whereas traditional
Jews focus on the love for fellow Jews, sometimes neglecting
the universal love for all people; less traditional and more
modern Jews sometimes focus on the love for non-Jews,
neglecting the special love Jews should have for each other.
We must increase our love for Jews *and* for non-Jews. We
require a restatement and renewal of a traditional Jewish religious humanism that begins with a special, fervent love for
fellow Jews and extends to an open and unabashed love for
all people.

MYSTIC GOALS
Love for God, D'vekut

The ultimate goal of Jewish mysticism is expressed in a
number of ways, the most common expression being *d'vekut* –
"cleaving" to God with a loving awareness of the divine
presence. *D'vekut* means a love for God so intense that
it resists the slightest separation, and the metaphor often
used to characterize it is the passionate love between man
and woman. Such loving God-consciousness is, the mystics
teach, by its very nature, blissful.

The supreme mystic attainment for a person is to achieve
constant *d'vekut* without a moment's cessation, for all twenty-
four hours of the day. When, by devoted spiritual practice
with self-sacrifice, a person becomes established in *d'vekut*,
he attains divine vision and his eyes behold his Maker; he
sees that everything in the world vibrates with divine
vitality. He tangibly senses and experiences God's presence

everywhere and all creation shines with the radiance of divine glory. When a person is in God's presence at all times, when he tastes at every moment the beauty, sweetness, and holiness of the *Shechinah* (the immanent Divine Presence), he lives in a world of bliss and joy that surpasses any bodily or worldly pleasure and he fulfills the purpose of his life in this world.

Love for Humanity and an Open Heart

Although it is rarely expressed explicitly, another mystic goal is love for humanity and for each individual person. Jewish mysticism transforms the mind and the heart; a Jewish mystic has an expanded consciousness and an open heart. Just as the soul yearns for *d'vekut* and unity with God, it also yearns for *d'vekut* and mystic unity with all other souls. The mystics teach what most of us know intuitively: that closeness to people and closeness to God are intimately related. But the deepest truth of this intuition and insight is only revealed in a mystic perspective.

THE MYSTIC PATH

To attain mystic goals, a person must engage as much as possible in *continuous* spiritual practice, so that she trains herself to remember God and to focus on God's presence at every moment and in every activity. Continuous practice leads to continuous God-awareness. Whether engaged in "religious" activities, such as Torah study, prayer, meditation, and Shabbat observance, or in "worldly" activities, such as eating, working, conversing, and cleaning the house, the focus should always be on God. Someone who seeks mystic awareness should also labor constantly to deepen her devotion, piety, and fervor, for what is necessary is not only continuity but depth and fire. We will see in what follows that, together with spiritual practices such as Torah study and prayer, humanism – loving and helping people – is a vital part of the Jewish mystic path.

EXPANDING CIRCLES OF LOVE

The essence of mysticism is love for God that leads to direct spiritual experience; the essence of humanism is love for people. Judaism teaches that Jews should have a special love for fellow Jews, just as an individual has a special love and obligation for members of his family. Our love should expand in concentric circles: We should love our family foremost, our people next, and then all humanity.

When we are discussing not the specific Torah obligations that differ for each circle but a mystic viewpoint that makes the highest demands (*lifnim mishurat hadin*[a]), the goal is to love most broadly and fully. If this ultimate goal and the image of concentric circles are understood, teachings of the mystics and rabbis that refer specifically to love for fellow Jews may often be applied more broadly to love for humanity; let the reader remember this as we proceed.

The two basic Torah teachings about love for people are similar: "You shall love your neighbor as yourself"[2] and "You shall love the stranger as yourself, for you were strangers in the land of Egypt"[3]. Many traditional commentators interpret the commandment to love one's neighbor as applying to fellow Jews, some interpret it as applying to all people. Rabbi Joseph Kimhi, in *Sefer HaBrit*, writes: "'You shall love your neighbor as yourself' does not refer only to Jews ... 'Your neighbor'

[a.] see the Glossary for unfamiliar terms

means someone like you, who is living like you in society with others, and all the nations are included."[4]   Whichever way we interpret this verse about loving our neighbor, we must love both neighbor and stranger, both Jew and non-Jew. Rabbi Elimelech of Lizensk, the great early hasidic rebbe and mystic, taught:

> The *tzaddik* (holy individual) loves God and also every person in the world, as Rabbi Yohanan said: "No one ever preceded me in offering the blessing of peace as a greeting, not even a gentile in the marketplace. "... though certainly not all loves are equal and the same, for a Jew's love for a fellow Jew is more complete than his love for a non-Jew.[5]

More recently, Rabbi Abraham Isaac Kook, the first chief rabbi of Israel, who was a great mystic and lover of humanity, wrote:

> I love all people. I am not able not to love all people and all nations. I desire from my deepest depths that all be raised to glory, that all be fully brought to perfection. My love for the Jewish people is more fervent and deeper, but the inner desire expands and spreads outward in a powerful love for all.[6]

He also wrote:

> My love for all God's creations, for all reality is great. Far be it from me to allow even the slightest dislike or hatred for God's creatures into my heart. I feel within me great love for all living creatures, especially for humans, and, on a higher level, for the children of Israel, and, on even higher levels, for those who revere God, who keep the Torah and *mitzvot* [commandments], how much more still for Torah sages. I do not want the honor of any human diminished. I want all to be elevated, all to be honored, all to be lifted up and brought to glory ....[7]

THE HISTORY OF JEWISH MYSTIC HUMANISM

Judaism has had arguably four great periods of dynamic and creative life: the time of the Torah (the Bible); the time of the ancient rabbis of the Talmud and *Midrash*; the time of the development of the Kabbalah in 16th century Israel; and the time of the early Hasidic Movement, which began in 18th century Eastern Europe and continues until today. Another important and vital movement, the Musar Movement[a], began in 19th century Eastern Europe and also continues into the present. The Torah, the ancient rabbis, the Kabbalah, and the Hasidic and Musar movements all provide valuable teachings about mystic humanism.

THE TORAH
An Image of God

It is ancient Jewish teaching that love for God must be expressed in love for our fellow humans and that serving God mainly consists in serving fellow humans. This teaching appears at the very beginning of the Book of Genesis in the account of the creation of man. This tale is the basis for the mystic humanistic viewpoint, as the following original insight will show.

The story of humanity's creation[8] portrays God as, so to

[a.] a pietistic movement among non-hasidic traditional Jews that emphasizes ethics and character development

speak, a man who scoops up clay from the ground and sculpts a little man in his own image, a small model of himself. But what actual human activity is being pictured here? This, of course, is a parable – God is not a man scooping up dirt – and every parable is based on something in real life. What real-life scene is the basis for this graphic parable of God's action? It is that of a sculptor who works with clay to produce a little image of a man. And in the world of ancient Israel, as in the rest of early antiquity, the actual context of such sculpting of human figurines was the age-old trade of – the idol-maker!

Is not this astonishing and even breath-taking, that the parable used for God's activity in creating humanity is an idol-maker? Isn't the Torah vehemently against idolatry? The meaning behind this story is, however, as important as it is radical, for the Torah makes a claim that turns the views of the idolaters on their heads.

In ancient times, idol-makers took clay, stone, or metal and constructed a human-like figure, which they said was the image of the god, made in their own human image. The Torah inverts this story and says: This is the way man was originally formed– with God fulfilling the part of the idol-maker! Out of clay He created a man, a small version of Himself, made "in His own image." The Hebrew word for "image," tzelem, used in the story of Adam's creation and in the phrase "divine image," tzelem elohim, is the same word employed elsewhere in the Torah for an idol.[9]

Although God is pictured as an idol-maker, this story contains a radical anti-idolatry message. The idolaters made statues, which they said were the images of their god, and to win the god's favor they ritually served and worshiped the idol. But the Torah story of man's creation out of clay, yet in God's image, teaches the very opposite: that idols of clay and stone are false and empty. Idolatry demeans human dignity by making people worship a lifeless object and it misrepresents

the nature of the living God. The idolaters say that the piece
of sculpted clay is the image of a god; it is to be served and
worshiped, bowed down to and revered. What does the
Torah say is the "idol," the true "image of God," which
should have our utmost respect and reverence? It is Man
himself. So the true worship of God is not the ritual temple
service of a lifeless image, devoid of ethics and with no
necessary link to justice and mercy. The true worship of God
is the love, service, and "worship" of living human beings,
who are veritably "in His image." This exciting insight into
the Genesis story is not an interpretation being read into the
text. It is the real meaning of the story.

The Torah is astonishingly bold in using the parable of an
idol-maker to portray God's creation of man. And the lesson
conveyed through this startling device is profound. The
essential teaching is that the love and worship of God are
best expressed through love of humankind. Moreover, the
statement that man is in the "image" of God contains a deep
mystic truth: God is not only far away in heaven and
separated from us. He appears on earth before our eyes in the
form of our fellow human beings. We see from this insight
into the Genesis story of man's creation that love for humanity
as the essence of Judaism and a belief in the divine dignity of
humanity were not invented later by the rabbis. They are
found at the beginning of the Torah and at its very heart.

The Founders of Judaism

Let us briefly consider the humanism of two of the
founders of Judaism and fathers of the Jewish people –
Abraham and Moses.

Abraham

The Torah says that God chose Abraham, the father of the Jewish people, because of his moral character and ethical behavior: "For I know him, that he will command his children and his household after him, and they shall keep the way of the Lord, to do righteousness and justice."[10] The Jewish tradition considers Abraham to be the symbol of compassion and love; the rabbis especially focused on his exceptional hospitality, as seen in the story of his receiving three angels disguised as humans.[11] Abraham's love included the wicked, and he pleaded with God to spare the people of Sodom.[12] One of the main teachings of traditional Jewish humanism is the essential link between religion and morality. The child-sacrifice practiced in Abraham's time was an extreme case of religion's separation from morality. In the story of Abraham's "near-sacrifice" of his son Isaac[13], God revealed to the world, through Abraham, the humanistic teaching that His worship never involves cruelty.

Moses

Moses's passion for justice and his compassion for the oppressed motivated his mission to free his fellow Jews from Egyptian slavery. But his justice and compassion were universal. After slaying an Egyptian overseer who was viciously beating a Hebrew slave, Moses fled to Midian. As soon as he arrived, he came to the aid of seven Midianite shepherd girls, whom some shepherds were chasing from the well where the girls had brought their flocks. Moses also watered the girls' flocks, showing he was compassionate as well as just.[14] So, Moses's concern for the weak and the oppressed included non-Jews too. Later, when he returned to Egypt and led the exodus of the Jews, he took along a great "mixed multitude" of gentiles, who fled with them. God revealed to the world through Moses that His true nature, His personality, so to speak, is loving and compassionate. He transmitted to Moses on Mount Sinai the Attributes of Divine Mercy (which we will discuss further on). Moses taught the people of Israel that God's worship is based on love, for God commanded the Jews, through Moses, to "love the Lord your God with all your heart, with all your soul, and with all your might"[15], to "love your neighbor as yourself"[16], and to "love him [the stranger] as yourself, for you were strangers in the land of Egypt."[17]

THE TEACHINGS OF THE ANCIENT RABBIS

The ancient rabbis developed the Torah's teaching of love for humanity. One way they did this was by drawing out the implications of the tales about Abraham and Moses.

About Abraham's Humanism

The ancient rabbis say about the verse "And the Lord appeared to him [Abraham] by the terebinths of Mamre,"[18] that Abraham had there a prophetic vision of God. Then, while he was having the divine vision, three angels disguised as men appeared at his tent. When confronted with a choice between his conversation with God and his three "human" visitors, the rabbis say that Abraham asked God to "wait" while he went to receive the three men: He showed them hospitality and served them a meal. The rabbis derived from this that "receiving guests is greater than receiving the *Shechinah*, the Divine Presence," in a prophetic vision or in prayer.[19] They also say that the angels appeared to Abraham as idol-worshiping Arab nomads[20].

Another way to view the rabbis' teaching is that when God conversed with Abraham, the *Shechinah* appeared to him without form and when God came to him as the three visitors, the *Shechinah* appeared to him with form as three men. This teaches a lesson in mystic humanism: Abraham left a direct prophetic experience of God for a mediated experience because he knew that receiving humans in the divine image was not only like but, in certain respects, even greater, than receiving the Divine Presence. He knew that God preferred that he care for people first, even idol-worshiping Arabs.

About Moses's Humanism

In another Torah tale, Moses, Aaron, and all the elders of Israel graciously received Moses's gentile father-in-law, Jethro, when he visited the Jews in the Sinai Desert, and they gave a feast in his honor. The rabbis again derived from this that "receiving a fellow human is like receiving the Divine Presence."[21]

Although Moses is mentioned as receiving Jethro, he is not mentioned in the feast scene, and the rabbis ask where he was during the feast. They answer that Moses, who was the greatest and therefore the humblest of people, was standing and serving while the others sat and ate. The rabbis say that Moses learned this behavior from Abraham – the greatest person of his generation – who served his three lowly guests.[22] In spiritual leadership, the greater serves the lesser. Why? Because the "lesser" also manifests the Divine Presence, the *Shechinah*.

Love and the Golden Rule:
Hillel and Rabbi Akiba

A famous story about Hillel, the greatest rabbi of ancient times, tells that a gentile once came to him and said, "Rabbi, I would like to convert to Judaism, but only if you can teach me the whole Torah while I am standing on one leg." Hillel taught him the Golden Rule, saying, "The essence of the Torah is: Do not do to others what you would not like done to you. The rest is commentary; but go home and study it."[23] In a parallel story, when Rabbi Akiba is asked by a simple Jew what the Torah's essence is, he answers that it is to love your neighbor as yourself. Then he explains using examples of the Golden Rule, such as, if you do not want your neighbor to harm your property, you must not harm your neighbor's property.[24]

The ancient rabbis considered the Golden Rule as the "rule of thumb" to fulfill the Torah's commandment to love your neighbor *as yourself*.[25] How do you know how to love your neighbor? By realizing that your neighbor is *as yourself*, by reflecting on how you would want to be treated if you were in her place. The negative Golden Rule – not doing to others what you would not want done to you, not to hate or to harm – is the beginner's lesson; the positive Golden Rule – treating others as you would want them to treat you, to love and to help – is the advanced lesson.[26]

This Hillel story is so familiar to Jews that they may neglect to see how radical it is. What happened to love of God? How can love of neighbor be "the whole Torah"? The answer is that Hillel so closely associated love of God with love of people – that a person should love God *by* loving people – that the former did not even have to be explicitly mentioned. Hillel's approach was thoroughly humanistic.

Hillel did not mean that the gentile should obey the Golden Rule only if he converted to Judaism. The Golden

Rule is for everyone to obey. And when a person follows the Golden Rule, she must also apply it to all humans, regardless of any distinctions, for its essential logic is unrestrictive and open: Treat the other person as you would want her to treat you. For example, if a Jew would want a non-Jew to treat her fairly and compassionately, when she is in need, that is how she must treat a non-Jew.

Humanity in God's Image and Mystically One: Rabbi Akiba and Ben Azzai

Ben Azzai agreed with his contemporary and comrade, Rabbi Akiba, that love of neighbor is a great principle of the Torah, but he claimed it is based on an even greater principle: that humans are created in God's image.[27] Akiba accepted this too, for he also taught: "Beloved is man because he is created in the image of God."[28] If taken seriously, this concept has a mystic meaning – that God is mysteriously present in the form of our fellow humans. Ben Azzai elsewhere clarifies his mystic view, when he explains with a parable the commandment against taking revenge or holding a grudge. He says:

> It is written: "Do not take revenge or bear a grudge against the children of your people, [the verse continues: but you shall love your neighbor as yourself; I am the Lord[29]]," for how can a person take revenge or bear a grudge against another person? It is like someone who is cutting meat that he is holding in his hand: If the knife accidentally slips and he cuts his hand, would he revenge that hand by cutting the other one?[30]

This simple parable expresses a belief in a mystic unity among people that is the basis for loving others and for not taking revenge or bearing a grudge against those who hurt or harm you. If someone harms you, how can you retaliate, for you would only be harming yourself!

The ancient rabbis, following the Torah's lead, taught the mystic view that people are formed in the divine image and that they are mystically one. Therefore, a person who seeks perfection must love even those who hate, hurt, or harm him. But this teaching relates only to personal not national matters and does not deny the need for justice and judgment.

Cleaving to God by Imitating His Loving Attributes

The tradition teaches that the mystic aspect of loving people is based on their being in the image of God and manifesting the *Shechinah;* therefore, loving and cleaving to them is like loving and cleaving to God. The ancient rabbis also teach, from another perspective, that the best way to cleave to God in *d'vekut* is by imitating His loving nature and attributes. Their comment on the Torah commandment to "cleave to Him" is: "cleave to His attributes of mercy."[31]

After the sin of the Golden Calf, Moses again ascended Mount Sinai and pleaded with God, "Make known to me Your ways, that I may know You, and so that I may find favor in Your sight."[32] Moses asked God to reveal to him His true personality, who He really is. God passed before Moses and made known His ways by calling out His essential character and nature: "The Lord, the Lord, a God merciful and gracious [giving], patient, and abundant in loyal love; keeping faith to the thousandth generation, bearing [forgiving] sin, iniquity, and transgression ...." The ancient rabbis counted thirteen aspects of God's mercy in this sentence, and called them The Thirteen Attributes of God's Mercy. Their essence is that God is loving, giving, patient, and forgiving. The Jewish tradition teaches that God, who is merciful and giving, is also a jealous

God, who judges and is wrathful against evil and evildoers. But His judgmental side is only the outside, for His inner nature is always love.[33]

God's revelation of His Thirteen Attributes of Mercy is one of the most important teachings in Judaism, but it is neglected. The most important Torah verses are that we should love the one God with all our heart, soul, and might[34]; and that we should love our neighbor as ourself[35]. The essence of Judaism is to love God and people. But a verse of equal importance is the Thirteen Attributes of Mercy, which tells us that God loves us.

The ancient rabbis teach that we should cleave to God by imitating His merciful attributes. They say: "Be like Him: As He is merciful, so should you be merciful; as He is giving, so should you be giving" (and so on for the other attributes). A few comments about these divine attributes that we should imitate:

God is loving (also translated as "merciful" or "compassionate").

God is gracious (better translated as "giving"); the rabbis say that, like God, we should give freely to all, even to those who are unworthy[36], without expecting any return.[37]

God is patient.

God is "abundant in loyal love"; Hillel said this means that we should judge others favorably.[38]

God is also forgiving, and so should we be.

By imitating God's loving attributes, by being compassionate, giving, patient, and forgiving, we cleave to God.

The Story of the Two Brothers

A beautiful rabbinic story[39] expresses the Jewish view that love between people reveals the Divine Presence. The story explains how the site for the ancient

Temple in Jerusalem was chosen in the time of King David.

There were two gentile[40] brothers who lived on adjacent farms, for when their father had passed away he had divided his land equally between them. One brother was married, with children; the other brother was single. It was the end of harvest time and both brothers' fields were dotted with heaps of grain.

One night, the single brother was sitting in his house and he thought to himself, "My brother is married and has to provide for all of his family; he has many mouths to feed. I'm alone and can support myself without much difficulty. I'll go and take some sheaves of grain from my heap and add them to a heap in his field. It will make things much easier for him. I'll go secretly at night so as not to embarrass him. I can make a few trips tonight, and I'll bring some more tomorrow night." So he went out in the middle of the night into his field, took some sheaves of grain on his shoulder, went to his brother's field, and put the grain in one of his brother's heaps.

Meanwhile, his brother was sitting in his house, and said to his wife, "My brother is at his farm all alone. He doesn't have, as I do, the joys and comforts of a family – a loving wife, and children .... His main happiness is his work, seeing that his farm is successful. We have enough to feed our family. I'll go and take some of our grain and put it in a heap in his field. He won't realize that someone has added to his heap. It will make him happy to feel that his farm is productive." So he got up, in the dark of the night, went out into his field, took some sheaves of grain on his shoulder, then went to his brother's field and put the grain in one of his brother's heaps.

The next day each brother discovered, to his surprise, that his and his brother's heaps were the same size as the day before, and they could not understand what had happened. Both brothers repeated their deeds on the next night, and on the next day again discovered that the heaps were still the same size. They were at a loss to understand what had happened.

But on the third night, as the brothers were again bringing sheaves of grain into each other's fields, they met at the border between their farms. When each saw

the other and realized what he was doing, they understood what had happened and why, and they fell on each
other's necks weeping, because of their love for each
other.
    And God chose that spot as the site where the Holy
Temple would be built.

That the site of the Temple, the center of Jewish worship
and prayer, and the place where God chose to dwell and to
reveal Himself, was selected because of an exceptional example
of human love is remarkable. The lesson is both humanistic
and mystic: God reveals Himself in human love and in
the merit of human love He reveals Himself in worship
and prayer. The *mutual* love between two *gentile* brothers
portrayed in the story has a messianic aspect – looking
forward to a time of universal love, when the rebuilt Temple
in Jerusalem will be "a house of prayer for all peoples."[41]

THE KABBALAH: RABBI MOSHE
CORDOVERO'S *PALM TREE OF DEBORAH*

The Kabbalah, which is primarily focused on mystic theology and heavenly matters, offers less in regard to mystic
humanism. Its most important humanistic teachings are in
the area of kabbalistic ethics. A number of great kabbalists
applied their mystic theology to ethics, most prominently,
Rabbi Moshe Cordovero, in his book *The Palm Tree of
Deborah (Tomer Devorah)* Rabbi Cordovero offers insights
into two major perspectives of mystic humanism: first, that
one cleaves to God by imitating His loving attributes, and
second, that Jews share a mystic oneness.
    In *The Palm Tree of Deborah*, Rabbi Cordovero discusses
each of the divine attributes of mercy in turn and explains
how it is a model for our ethical behavior. He teaches that
when a Jew imitates a divine attribute, he is channeling that

divine trait into the world and, so to speak, sharing in the divine life.[42]

As to the mystic unity of the Jewish people, Rabbi Cordovero states: "The souls [of all Jews] are united [and included in each other], for each person has a part of the soul of all others."[43] Therefore, he says, Jews are commanded "you shall love your neighbor as yourself," because "he is actually he," that is, your neighbor is, in part, actually you.[44]

HASIDISM: RABBI ISRAEL BAAL SHEM TOV

The mystic and humanistic perspective taught in the Torah, and taught by the ancient rabbis and by the kabbalists was further developed in Hasidism by Rabbi Israel Baal Shem Tov, founder of the Hasidic movement, and the hasidic rebbes who followed him. The Baal Shem Tov was able to revive Jewish mysticism in the 18th century because he was both a mystic and a humanist. He attained exalted mystic spiritual levels and he powerfully attracted the Jewish people to him by his devoted love for them.

A Mystic Love for Fellow Jews

The Zohar (the main book of the Kabbalah) says that God, the Torah, and Israel (the Jewish people) are one. God, those who worship Him, and the scripture that connects them to Him, are mystically one. The Baal Shem Tov said that a Jew must have three loves: love of God, love of the Jewish people, and love of the Torah.[45] Since the Torah and Israel are one with God, love of the Torah and love of the Jewish people have, he said, a mystic meaning: A Jew loves the Torah because it is God's Word and she loves other Jews not merely because they share her ethnicity but because they are God's people. The Jewish people have dedicated their peoplehood to God in a special way. One of their contributions to the world will be to teach other nations how to sanctify their nationhood. Because the Jewish people, as a people, are mystically connected to God, when a Jew loves fellow Jews, she is, in a special way, loving God.

The Baal Shem Tov's Spiritual Levels

Although he was a great Torah scholar, the Baal Shem Tov's primary spiritual practice was prayer. But his mysticism was also rooted in the core Jewish teaching that love of God is best expressed in love for fellow humans. A tradition reports that the Besht[a] said it was revealed to him that he reached his exalted mystic spiritual levels not because of his talmudic study or erudition but because of his fervent prayer, offered with self-sacrifice[46], for he was willing to expire for the *kavvanah* (the God-ward intention) of the prayers.

The Baal Shem Tov taught his followers to pray with devotion and fervor. But he also taught them that by lovingly helping fellow Jews with self-sacrifice, they would reach higher levels of soul-revelation[47]– and mystic realization – than by the deepest solitary prayer or meditation on Godliness (divinity).[48]

Paralleling the tradition that the Besht attained great heights spiritually because of his fervent praying, there is another tradition that he attained his spiritual levels because of his devoted teaching of children when, as a young man, he was an assistant teacher in an elementary religious school.[49] One story tells that he loved the children so much that he hugged and kissed them.[50] Another story tells that he risked

---

[a.] an acronym for Baal *Shem* Tov

his life to confront and kill a wolf that threatened children whom he was leading to school.[51]

The Baal Shem Tov's passionate praying expressed his self-sacrificing love for God and his protection of the children expressed his self-sacrificing love for people. By self-sacrificing love for God and for people, a person dissolves the narrow limitations of his ego to reveal his soul and is elevated to mystic consciousness.

People often think that becoming a mystic implies separating from others and concentrating primarily on prayer and meditation. Separation may occasionally be necessary for spiritual development; the Baal Shem Tov served God in seclusion for a while. But the Baal Shem Tov's teachings and the tales about him show that serving humanity also leads to spiritual attainment and is an essential part of the mystic path.

Other Examples of the Baal Shem Tov's Love for People

Two tales provide insight into the Baal Shem Tov's love for people and its mystic meaning.

Love Him More

> The son of a religious man strayed from the fold and became a nonbeliever. The distraught father went to the Baal Shem Tov, desperately seeking advice for what to do. The Besht told the father, "Love him more." The father did so and, as a result, his son abandoned his atheism and returned to God.[52]

One reason the Baal Shem Tov advised the father as he did is that he believed in a mystic unity among people, with the Divine Presence dwelling between them (as in the teaching of Ben Azzai, see previously, p.20). When someone else withdraws from me, I, to prevent the Divine Presence from departing, have to draw closer to him and "fill the empty space" (see further on, p.47).

How Could I Wait?

The Baal Shem Tov was once in a certain city whose rabbi was a great Torah scholar. This rabbi did not believe in the Baal Shem Tov, but, having heard the extra-ordinary things people were saying about him and the miracles he was performing, very much wanted to meet the Besht and talk with him. However, he was reluctant to lower his own dignity by going to the Besht. He felt that since he was the rabbi of the city it was proper that the Baal Shem Tov come to him, and visit him in his house. When they reported this to the Baal Shem, he said, "Not only doesn't he come to me to welcome me to his city, he wants me to go to him."

Finally, the rabbi went to the Baal Shem Tov, but when he came to his room, the Besht was not there, for he had gone to the outhouse. An agunah[a] was also waiting in the Besht's room. When the Besht returned to his room, he picked up the vessel with water to wash his hands [required by Jewish law after going to the bathroom]. But before he could do so, the woman immediately accosted him; she wept and pleaded with him hysterically that he tell her [by means of his holy spirit] about her husband– was he alive or dead? if alive, where was he? She did not even allow the Besht to wash his hands. Finally he said to her that her husband was alive, and in a certain city, and that she should go there and she would find him.

After she left, the rabbi, who had observed all this, said to the Baal Shem Tov, "If your words were prophecy, shouldn't you first have washed your hands, and then

---

[a.] a woman whose husband is missing and who, according to Jewish religious law, cannot remarry

spoken to her in a state of [ritual] cleanliness?" The Baal Shem Tov replied, "If you came into your house and saw that two chickens had gotten in from outside, and were jumping up on a table on which there were expensive glass objects, would you wait to wash your hands first before you chased them out? Because meanwhile, the glass would be broken. And I, praise God, see [with the holy spirit] that her husband is walking around in that city, and he is actually before my eyes– just as you would see the glass objects on the table and the chickens. And you are standing there and able to do something. So I see her husband there, and she is here, in anguish, weeping and crying out in front of me– can I wait until I wash my hands first? Every minute her soul is shattering into a thousand pieces and she is dying a thousand times. How could I wait?"[53]

This tale tells that the Besht, with his holy spirit, could see at a distance, but his deeper achievement was that he could see and share the suffering of someone who was standing in front of him. We can strive to attain *that* quality. Opening our heart to other people's pain is an expression of mystic identity and oneness.

THE MUSAR MOVEMENT: RABBI NOSON TZVI FINKEL OF SLOBODKA

Hasidism is not the only pietistic movement in Judaism. The Musar movement, which emphasizes ethics and character development, can also teach us about loving and serving humanity. Rabbi Noson Tzvi Finkel, the Elder of Slobodka, one of the great early Musar teachers, based his spiritual life on imitating God's love for all His creatures– as expressed in His attributes of mercy. According to Rabbi Noson Tzvi, the essence of what we know about God is that He is all-powerful, that He creates and directs the universe; and that He is all-good, for everything He does is only from love of His creatures. His goodness to people flows continually and without cease, every hour and every minute. That, says the Slobodker, should be the model for our actions – to be loving and good to all the people in the world, without cease, as much as it is in our power to do.[54]

Love for humanity and an open heart are goals of Jewish mystical practice. The tales about the Baal Shem Tov show his open heart. Rabbi Noson Tzvi Finkel is also an exceptional model of a person with an open heart. The following description of him is taken from a book about the most famous Musar teachers:

> [The rabbis divide the *mitzvot* into two categories – those that concern the relationship between a person and God and those that concern the relationship between one person and another.] Rabbi Noson Tzvi made the relations between a person and his fellow the foundation of his service of God. In this, he reached the pinnacle of achievement. He constantly emphasized in his teaching that humans are created in God's image and that helping or hurting another human is like helping or hurting the Divine Presence. He worked on himself until this perspective was so firmly established within him that it was reflected in all his actions in practice.[55]
>
> Rabbi Noson Tzvi believed that a person's heart should continually flow with love and kindness and that one should use every opportunity to speak kind words and to bless people. He especially emphasized greeting people warmly, because he believed it gave people *nahas*, deep gratification, that it won their heart and drew them closer to him.
>
> Rabbi Noson Tzvi Finkel was not satisfied with merely doing good to people when an opportunity arose, he actively sought occasions to do good. Whenever he did a favor or an act of kindness, he did it with extreme care and reverence for even the smallest details, because he was doing it for a human created in the image of God![56] He taught that no matter how well you treat other

AN OPEN HEART   31

people it will never be enough. Since they are actual
images of God, they deserve more than you could ever
give them.[57] He bestowed on everyone he met all of his
goodness. If there was no opportunity to do good for
someone in practice, he expressed his earnest wish to
have done the favor if it had only been possible.

He would always bless everyone and pray for everyone. As a yeshivah teacher in his younger days, his
custom on Sabbaths and holidays was that after the
morning prayers he would pass among the students,
going row by row, bench by bench, to bless them with
"Good Shabbos" or "Good Yom Tov" (holiday). He gave
these blessings intently and with feeling. Sometimes he
would sit by the window in his home and shower blessings and prayers on every passerby! Once, when he was
walking by the home of the Rosh Yeshivah (headmaster),
accompanied by one of his students, he called out,
"Good morning!" although there no one was there.
When his student became confused at seeing no one
there, Rabbi Noson Tzvi said to him, "I've never understood why people feel they should only greet and bless
others whom they see. Why not bless everyone in the
house even when you don't see them?"[58]

Rabbi Noson Tzvi was especially attentive to the
sick. Whenever he heard that someone was sick, he
immediately asked for the person's name and the name
of his or her mother [needed for a traditional prayer for
the sick] and began to plead before God for her recovery.
Once, when he was visiting in Jerusalem, he was sitting
in the waiting room of a dentist's office and heard the
groans of someone inside whose tooth was being pulled.
Rabbi Noson Tzvi anxiously expressed his sympathy for
the person's distress and pain and immediately stood up
to pray for him.

Rabbi Noson Tzvi extended his love and reverence
to non-Jews as well as to Jews, for he said that all
humans are precious, created in God's image and
beloved of God. Once, when he was walking on a small
street on the outskirts of Slobodka, in the company of his
son-in-law, Rabbi Eizik, he noticed that a new non-
kosher cafe had opened up at the end of the street. He

enthusiastically expressed his happiness about this to his son-in-law, because he had always been troubled by the fact that in this outlying area there was no place for gentile travelers to rest and relax as soon as they entered the town, so they could have something to eat or drink and satisfy their thirst or hunger![59]

A book about Rabbi Noson Tzvi says:

> He loved people with an extraordinary and excessive love, a love without restraints; he had a limitless affection for humanity – for any human, regardless of who or what he was. He was also extremely sensitive to any humiliation of any person and he fully participated in other people's suffering. The source for these qualities is that he saw in people the image of God, a part of God from Above. Every human was, for him, like Adam – a creation of God's own hands – before his sin and fall ... whose holiness is part of the nature of every human even after the Sin, even after the sins of all later generations and all the terrible descents and falls.[60]
>
> [According to Jewish law, it is a *mitzvah* to accompany people a short distance when they leave your presence.] Rabbi Noson Tzvi Finkel would occasionally walk along the platform to "accompany" trains leaving the station. He would accompany a Gypsy wagon as it left the town. Why? because all these people – Jews and gentiles alike – were in the image of God and deserved the greatest honor![61]
>
> Rabbi Noson Tzvi taught that love of people is the way to understand and approach love of God. He said that without fulfilling and understanding the relationship between a person and his fellow it is impossible to have any true understanding of the relationship between a person and God.
>
> His students once asked him, "Why is it that in most of your talks you constantly emphasize the 'between a person and his fellow,' in a direct and concrete way, while, it seems to us, you always approach the 'between a person and God' indirectly, by way of 'between a person and his fellow'? Only in rare instances do you discuss

heavenly matters in your talks, giving the kind of lengthy explanations that you give when you discuss 'a person and his fellow.'"

His reply was short but deep. "Look at how difficult it is for us to achieve the proper feeling to fulfill our ethical and moral obligations to our closest friends who are always with us. Although 'what is hateful to you' [the first part of the Golden Rule] is so simple and clear to us, yet every minute we are failing with the 'don't do to your fellow (friend)'[the second part of the Golden Rule]. Despite all our efforts, we still have no conception of the 'image of God' that is in humans, which obligates us to honor each person and to recognize his greatness. If so, is it not even more difficult to acquire the proper understanding and feeling to fulfill the 'between a person and God'? And how far we are from it! If we have not perfectly comprehended the 'between a person and his fellow,' namely, the image of God in other people, which is something 'near to you and in your mouth, to do it,'[62] how can we conceive even the least bit the awesome feeling needed to fulfill the 'between a person and God'?"[63]

In his answer, the Elder of Slobodka humbly included himself with his students, as if he too failed to fully respect the image of God in people and to fulfill the Golden Rule in dealing with them; but he was far advanced in his spiritual relationships to people and to God. What his answer conveys is that a person should concentrate first on what is close to him and before his eyes, namely, other people, as a path to attaining what is more difficult and less accessible, namely, a true and powerful relationship to God. It is also implicit in his words that a person should concentrate first on honoring others as a path to loving them.

Rabbi Noson Tzvi Finkel's love for people grew from his determination to treat others as divine images. By taking seriously, as he did, that humans are in God's image, a person becomes able to act on that belief in his daily life. Rabbi Noson Tzvi Finkel also taught that only by imitating God's love and mercy does a person manifest his own divine image (see p.59). Certainly, Rabbi Noson Tzvi Finkel was a radiant and holy tzaddik who revealed the divine image and who was like God in his overflowing love for all creatures. He movingly illustrates the mystic goal of an open heart. We should note that, as with any praise of holy people, the point of these tales about the Baal Shem Tov and about Rabbi Noson Tzvi Finkel is to encourage us not merely to appreciate their spiritual nobility but to emulate it.

ESSENTIAL TEACHINGS OF MYSTIC HUMANISM

We have reviewed the history of Jewish mystic humanism and have learned about humanity in the image of God and as manifesting the Shechinah, about the mystic unity of people, and about cleaving to God by imitating His loving attributes. We now come to the essence of the mystic view about love of neighbor. It is best expressed in two hasidic teachings that are little known and rarely discussed; they are brief but potent.

MYSTIC LOVE OF NEIGHBOR AS YOUR OWN SELF

The first major hasidic mystic teaching is this: The Torah says that you are to love your neighbor "as yourself."[64] Why? Because – say the hasidic mystics – your neighbor is yourself. That is the mystical understanding of the Torah verse. Loving a neighbor is not love of another but really love of yourself, for you and your neighbor are in essence one.[65] This hasidic teaching clarifies the significance of Ben Azzai's parable about not taking revenge when one hand accidentally hurts the other, and is similar but not identical to a kabbalistic insight previously mentioned (p.25). A hasidic book states: "All the souls (in their root) are one essence. Even when divided into parts, there exists in each part the whole essence. So a person's love of his neighbor is not love of another, but– love of himself."[66] Hasidim call this exalted level, of loving another in the same way that you love yourself, "essence-love" (*ahavah atzmit*), because you see all souls as part of the same divine essence and as extensions of yourself.[67]

LOVE OF YOUR NEIGHBOR *IS* LOVE OF GOD

The second major hasidic mystic teaching goes deeper than the first in focusing on the divine soul as a part of God. The oneness between you and your neighbor, the central part of each of your beings, is God. Jewish mysticism teaches that your essence and his essence, that is, your souls, are parts of God; and the one Soul, the one Self, that you share is God's *Shechinah*. Love of another is, then, also love of God, who is the Soul of all souls, the Self of all selves, that is, God's divine presence in this world, the *Shechinah*.

Rabbi Eliezer Papo writes in *Pele Yo'aitz:* "Do not worry about your [limited] 'self,' but about your real self, which is the Holy One, blessed be He, who is the Soul of the soul."[68]

The Baal Shem Tov taught:

"Love of Israel *is* love of God."[69]

"'You shall love your neighbor as yourself'[70] is the commentary and explanation of 'You shall love the Lord your God'[71], for every Jew contains within him a part of God from Above.[72] So when you love a fellow Jew, that is, his soul, his inner self, you are loving God.[73]

"When you grasp a part of the whole, you grasp the whole"[74]; and: "When you cleave to a part of the [divine] unity, you cleave to the unity."[75]

The Baal Shem Tov spoke of the true self or the soul as a "part" of God and as a "spark" of the *Shechinah*. The metaphor is of the *Shechinah* as a huge fire and each soul as a spark from the fire, sharing its essence. He taught: "When doing a kind act, your intention should be to be kind to the

Shechinah, that is, to the spark of the *Shechinah* in this particular person, because a person is a part of God from Above."[76]

When a person realizes his mystic identity with other people, his behavior toward them is profoundly affected. The Baal Shem Tov taught that a Jew should love every other Jew, even someone he never met before, and try, with self-sacrifice, to benefit him in any way possible.[77] He said that helping a fellow Jew with self-sacrifice, sacrifices your ego but reveals your soul (see p.26), since self-sacrifice reveals the spiritual reality that your soul (self) and his soul are in essence one. Rabbi Menachem Mendel Schneersohn, the late Lubavitcher Rebbe, said that you should help the other person with self-sacrifice because that is the way you help yourself. When someone is in need, it should touch your soul and you should act without calculations, just as you would act for yourself.[78] And since loving a fellow Jew is like loving God, just as one must love God with all one's heart, soul, and might, with self-sacrifice, so must one help another Jew.[79]

Even love of oneself is love of the *Shechinah*. The commandment is to love your neighbor *as yourself*. A person must learn to love himself or herself and to appreciate her own inner essence, her divine soul, her Godliness. The Torah commands us: "take great care of yourselves"[80]. Hillel taught that caring for oneself and one's body is honoring an image of God, and explained this teaching with the metaphor of a caretaker cleaning a statue of the king. Why does the Torah ordain that you care so diligently for yourself? because you are a part of God from Above.

LOVE FOR ESSENCE, LOVE FOR VIRTUE

Loving people for their essence, their soul, does not mean that one loves all people equally or that one makes no distinctions in love. There is a love for people's essence and another love according to their individuality and virtue. Essence-love requires helping people whenever possible and even self-sacrifice in certain circumstances. But just as there are concentric circles of love for family, nation, and humanity, there are concentric circles of love with regard to people's virtues, so that one loves individuals for their character and achievements, for their goodness and holiness.[81] One loves everyone, but one loves a *tzaddik* with a special love.

ATTAINING MYSTIC LOVE

Rabbi Eliyahu Dessler, a Musar teacher of the last generation, taught that giving to others opens our heart to love them.

> If one were only to reflect that *a person comes to love the one to whom he gives,* he would realize that the only reason the other person seems a stranger to him is because he has not yet *given* to him; he has not taken the trouble to show him friendly concern. If I give to someone, I feel close to him; I have a share in his being. It follows that if I were to start bestowing good upon everyone I come into contact with, I would soon feel that they are *all* my relatives, *all* my loved ones. I now have a share in them all; my being has extended into all of them.
>
> Someone who has been granted the merit to reach this sublime level can understand the command, "'You shall love your neighbor as yourself'" in its literal sense: 'As yourself': without distinction between you and him ... 'as yourself': in actual fact."[82] By giving to him of yourself you will find in your soul that you and he are indeed one; you will feel in the clearest possible manner that he really is to you *as yourself.*[83]

To increase one's mystic awareness, one should say to oneself, when giving to others and helping them, "Isn't this person in essence one with me? Isn't his soul a part of God just like my soul?"

One can only truly love God by loving people. And one can only reach the awesome level of being able to love another as oneself by loving God. Rabbi Tzadok HaCohen of Lublin writes: "No one can fulfill 'love your neighbor as yourself' except by attaining faith and d'vekut with God."[84]

Rabbi Shneur Zalman of Liadi, the first Lubavitcher Rebbe, said that only a person who focuses primarily on his soul and not on his body, on what is spiritual rather than what is worldly, can hope to attain and experience the mystic essence-love based in the unity of souls. Two individuals are two separate bodies but their souls are united; so only when a person puts his soul before his body can this spiritual reality of a unified essence become manifest.[85] A person who focuses on his body, will be selfish and egotistic; his love will be for himself, with none to spare for God or other people. A person who focuses on his soul will be selfless and self-sacrificing for others; he will find God within and have love for God, for people, and for his own true essence.

Rabbi Adin Steinsaltz said: When I look at the "I" of my body, I find the "I" of my soul, and when I look at the "I" of my soul, I find the "I" of God.[86] The highest spiritual level, even beyond the level where a person experiences himself as his soul, is where he nullifies even his independent, separate soul existence to merge with divinity and to be only a vessel for the "I" of God; then his love for others will be complete, essence-love.[87]

Mystic Vision: Looking at a Person's Soul

Rabbi Abraham Isaac Kook, the first chief rabbi of Israel, was a great mystic and lover of people. He loved even the socialist Zionist Jews, who were non-religious and often anti-religious, but who built Israel. Rabbi Kook said they were doing God's work.

> Once, the manager of a left-wing kibbutz was in Rabbi Kook's office. The Rabbi had heard that they were serving leavened bread at the kibbutz during Passover, so he asked him about it.
> The man tried to explain, "Rabbi, with all due respect, we are socialists. We can't be expected to adhere to these customs and observances. We're *totally* non-religious!"
> The Rabbi became agitated. He grabbed the man's arm and said to him, in a quavering voice full of passion, "You're not religious? *Never* say such a thing! *Of course* you're religious!"[88]

Rabbi Kook, being a holy man, only looked at a person's soul. And on the soul level, everyone's soul is always directly connected to God, it is a part of God, even if the person thinks that he is the world's greatest atheist.

When one looks at the other person's soul, one is able to love him.

A LOVING PERSON

Rabbi Shalom Noah Berzhovsky, the current Slonimer Rebbe in Jerusalem, paints a beautiful word picture, surely a self-portrait, of a loving person.

> His only goal in life is to be a loving and compassionate person. He builds his world on love, striving to love everyone in his heart and always seeking to help everyone in thought, speech, and deed. He arouses love in his mind, caresses with his gaze everyone he meets, and each word he speaks is like a healing balm and like a poultice on the heart of whomever hears it. All his thoughts are about how he can help another person. He is always soft and gentle, and even when he should be

hard, he forbears. He sees only the positive in others. He is always hopeful that everything will turn out for the good, because he knows that the Holy One, blessed be He, loves him and it is impossible that He would do him evil. He loves God and he loves all of God's creatures. He never becomes angry at others or at himself. His life is full of sweetness and meaning, for himself and for everyone around him, and only goodness and mercy pursue him all the days of his life.[89]

Beyond all the charity and kind deeds he performs, what sets apart a truly loving person is that his very essence is transformed into love ... so that he himself becomes a blessing. Everyone who comes in contact with him, or has dealings with him, or even sees him is blessed. Someone who is truly loving always feels for the other person, to whom he offers his whole heart. When his friend is being strangled by suffering and his spirit is choking, he fulfills the verse "I am with him in his trouble"[90], encouraging him and breathing hope into him. In times of happiness, he truly shares his friend's joy. A loving person bestows goodness on all who share his companionship and he gives to the other person his full attention, for he loves every Jew as much as his own body. By his very being and his presence he sheds his happy spirit on everyone near him and he imparts an atmosphere of love and friendship to his surroundings and a joyful feeling to all who come in contact with him. It seems as if he was created only to help other people. He shares in the expansiveness of the attribute of love, and love and kindness spread out from him to those far and near.[91]

LESSONS IN MYSTIC LOVE

Let us consider some implications of mystic humanism and how its teachings may be applied.

Anger and Patience

If we internalize the mystic view that all souls are really parts of one pervasive Soul, the *Shechinah*, we will never become angry at another person. If somebody begins to arouse your anger or gets angry with you, you should try to be patient, and think, "There is only one pervasive Soul, one 'I,' in both our bodies, in both her and me– the *Shechinah*. So with whom shall I get angry?" We can only be angry when we identify with the body. Instead of focusing on the different bodies, focus on the "I," the Soul of your souls. How can you be angry or feel hatred if you realize, "My essence is not my body but the *Shechinah* that is in both of us."

Not Judging Others and Forgiving Them Their Faults

One aspect of loving others is to forgive them for their sins and faults. The Baal Shem Tov taught that just as you forgive *yourself*, always finding excuses for yourself and *your* behavior, so should you find excuses for your neighbor.[92] A person who attains the high mystical state of essence-love spontaneously overlooks the other person's imperfections because he loves the other person just as he loves himself and one naturally overlooks one's own faults. Rabbi Nahum of Tchernobil taught:

> If someone sees something bad or evil in another person, he should hate the evil, but should love the other person's holy part [his soul], in the same way as he loves himself. The Baal Shem Tov said that a perfect *tzaddik*, who has no evil in him, sees no evil in others, for what we see in others is like a mirror: If your face is dirty, you see a dirty face in the mirror, but if your face is clean, you see nothing wrong; as you are, so you see. This is "you

shall love your neighbor as yourself" – "as yourself" means that if a person knows that he has faults, he does not on that account hate himself, although he hates the evil in him. He should act in the same way toward the other person, for does he not also have a part of God within him?[93]

Loving Enemies and The Wicked

How can we love someone who harms us or who acts as our enemy? If we recognize the mystic unity among souls, then, as Ben Azzai taught, we will not take revenge or bear a grudge against someone who harms us, just as your left hand would not "punish" your right hand that accidentally hurt it. Why should a person cause himself additional pain by retaliating against his neighbor?

Ben Azzai said that the great principle of love of neighbor rested on another, even more profound, principle: that man is made in the image of God. He emphasized this because some people perverted the commandment to love your neighbor "as yourself" to mean that if I am badly treated by you, I'll "love" you equally and treat you the same way. But if every human is in God's image, even if a person treats you badly, you do not respond in kind. Ben Azzai taught: "Do not treat any human with contempt"[94]; and the rabbis said: "You should not say: If I am treated with contempt, let him be shown contempt also, 'like me'; if I've been cursed by him, let him be cursed also, 'like me.' Rabbi Tanhuma said: If you have done so, know to whom you have shown contempt, for in the image of God made He man."[95]

The commandments not to take vengeance or bear a grudge and to love your neighbor are in the same verse (see p.20) and are intimately related. Many people know the Golden Rule, which is the rule to apply the commandment to love your neighbor as yourself. Few people, however, know the ancient rabbis' equally important rule to apply the commandment not to take revenge or bear a grudge.

> The rabbis said: What is considered revenge and what is bearing a grudge?
> If you say to your neighbor, "Lend me your scythe," and he refuses, and the next day he comes to you and says, "Lend me your spade," if you answer, "I won't lend it to you, just like you wouldn't lend your tool to me" – that is revenge. Therefore, the Torah says, "You shall not take revenge."
> And what is considered bearing a grudge? If you say to your neighbor, "Lend me your scythe" and he won't lend it to you, and the next day he comes and says, "Lend me your spade," if you answer, "Here, take it. I'm not like you, because you wouldn't lend your tool to me" – that is bearing a grudge. Therefore, the Torah says, "You shall not bear a grudge."[96]

What this means is that a person should return good for evil. When someone treats you badly, you should not only be ready to do him good, but you should not even remind him of what he did, as Leviticus 19:18 teaches: You should neither take revenge nor bear a grudge, but love your neighbor as yourself. This rule, explaining the meaning of not taking revenge or bearing a grudge, has many important applications in daily life.

God is loving and does good even to those who are unworthy and to those who are wicked. Immediately preceding the revelation of the Thirteen Attributes of Mercy, God said: "I will be gracious (giving) to whom I will be gracious and I will be merciful to whom I will be merciful."[97] Rabbi Meir interpreted this to mean that God will be giving and merciful even to those who are unworthy.[98] A High Holiday prayer says that God "is good and does good to the wicked and to the good." The ancient rabbis taught that we should imitate God's attributes, saying: "Be like Him: As He is merciful, so should you be merciful." Rabbi Meir clarified the extent of our obligation to be good, and taught: "Be like Him: As He returns good for evil, so should you return good for evil."[99]

The hasidic rebbes teach that when we love the other person's essence, his or her soul, it is immaterial whether he is righteous or wicked, a friend or an enemy, for, as with love of ourself, "love covers all sins."[100] Rabbi Dov Ber, the Maggid of Mezritch, was the Baal Shem Tov's great disciple and successor as leader of the Hasidic Movement.

> One night, it was the turn of Rabbi Elimelech of Lizensk, as a disciple of the Maggid, to attend to his master, so, as his Rebbe slept, he sat awake in the room next to his master's bedroom. In the middle of the night, Rabbi Dov Ber suddenly called to him and exclaimed, "Melech, Melech, do you hear what they're saying in the Heavenly Academy? that love of Israel means that one must love a completely wicked person as much as one loves a completely righteous person, a *tzaddik gamur!*"[101] (During sleep, Rabbi Dov Ber's soul ascended to heaven, where he heard what was being taught in the Heavenly Academy.)

Someone once asked Rabbi Shmelke of Nikolsburg, another great disciple of the Maggid of Mezritch, "How can I love wicked people?" Rabbi Shmelke replied, "You have to love the soul within them, because it is a part of God from Above. Have compassion for God, for the holy spark that is trapped within the Shells[a]."[102] That is, we should take pity on a person's divine essence, his Godly soul, which is being stifled by his evil exterior.

Rabbi Noson Tzvi Finkel's whole life was an attempt to imitate God's love and goodness to all creatures. He said that, like God, we must not differentiate between righteous and wicked, because God is good to all, causing His sun to shine on all alike and causing other natural forces to act for the

---

[a.] a kabbalistic expression for the evil forces that surround the soul, separating it from God

good of all, even for the wicked while they are being wicked. Therefore, like God, we must love and do good without expecting any return; we must be benevolent to the wicked too, even while they are abusing us.[103] Rabbi Noson Tzvi taught that we must treat everyone with the utmost love and respect because the most wicked person never loses his divine image. When Jacob met his wicked brother Esau, he said to him, "I have seen your face as if seeing the face of God."[104] Rabbi Noson Tzvi compared a sinful or wicked person to a sleeping king and said that even when asleep a king's honor is precious, because he is still the king and all must treat him as such.[105]

The hasidic rebbe, Rabbi Noson Netta of Chelm, said about Jacob's respectful greeting, of bowing before Esau[106]: "Esau represents the Other Side [Evil]. Our father Jacob did not bow before Esau but before the holy power, the spark that was within him, which is a part of God from Above. By bowing before this holy spark in Esau, Jacob added holiness to it and gave the holy spark power to overcome the evil in Esau."[107] The "holy spark," the "part of God from Above," is the soul, the "image of God."

When a good person acts humbly and shows love and respect for someone who has gone astray, he encourages that person to repent. We are told that Aaron the High Priest warmly greeted everyone, even a wicked and sinful person, until he would say: "How can I continue sinning? For how will I be able to look in Aaron's face when he greets me on the street?"

Rabbi Pinhas of Koretz, a great disciple of the Baal Shem Tov, reported his master's thoughts about how to deal with those who harm or hurt us:

> When someone abuses you and causes you suffering, you must make every effort to love him even more than before. There are three reasons for this: First, because you will be strongly tempted to hate him, and loving

your neighbor is a cardinal principle of the Torah. So you
must exert yourself to the utmost to overcome your evil
inclination and love him even more. Second, because of
your love for him, he will repent. So you must love even
wicked people, while hating their evil deeds. It is forbidden
to draw too close to them, however; you should love
them and perhaps this will bring them to repent. This is
what is written about Aaron: that he loved and pursued
peace, loved people and drew them to the Torah.[108] By
loving people he led them to repent, and drew them to
the Torah. Because when I love someone, he will also
love me, for "As water reflects a face, so does the heart of
a person reflect the heart of his fellow"[109]. And I hate his
evil deeds; so he also will begin to hate them and will
repent. [The story of the Besht advising a father to love
his straying son "more" is given in the text here to illustrate
this teaching; see this booklet, p.27.] Third, you must
love him more because the Congregation of Israel is a
chariot [vessel] for holiness, and when they are unified
and love each other, the Shechinah and all holiness dwell
among them. But when, God-forbid, there is any schism
between them, the holiness falls among the [evil] Shells,
which is terrible; so when a person sees that his fellow is
withdrawing from him, he must love him more and draw
even nearer to him to close the empty space.[110]

Although a person should love even wicked and sinful
people, he should not forget all caution and become too close
to them. One can bow respectfully to a wicked Esau's divine
image from a distance; it is dangerous to embrace him.
Showing love and respect to evil people does not imply
acting toward them in a way contrary to Torah wisdom. We
should be loving but also wise. Compassion for the wicked
does not negate justice. The rabbis wisely said: "He who is
compassionate to the cruel, will end up being cruel to the
compassionate."[111] Being overly lenient to a violent person,
for example, and letting him strike again is cruel to an innocent,
compassionate person who is his next victim. Also, love for
enemies and the wicked applies to personal, not to national,

enemies. Judaism does not countenance pacifism. Finally, there is no substitute for wisdom and no simple rule for balancing love and honor with prudence in responding to the wicked or enemies.

Identifying with Others' Suffering

The mystic goal is to identify with other people and to experience them as part of our self. A main motive for helping others is because we identify with their suffering.

The rabbis offer a striking parable of how God shares in human suffering, even the suffering of sinful people.

> A pregnant woman angered her mother, who went to stay on the upper floor. When the woman went into labor on the ground floor, and was crying out in pain below, her mother, hearing her cries, echoed them from above. Her neighbors said to her, "Why are you screaming? Are you giving birth with her?" She answered, "When my dear daughter is in labor and suffering, even though she angered me, can I bear her cries? So I cry out with her." So too does God share in the suffering of His daughter, Israel, even when He is angry at her.[112]

God shares in the suffering even of people who are being justly punished for their wickedness by the religious court. Rabbi Meir said that when a criminal is being put to death and hung, the Shechinah laments: "O, My head aches, My arms ache!" He concluded: If God suffers this way at the pain of the wicked, how much more so does He suffer at the pain of the righteous![113] The Torah says that the religious court should bury an executed criminal and not leave his body hanging overnight. Rabbi Meir explained this by a parable of a king who had his own twin hanged for a crime. But the king had the body taken down quickly, lest people say, "The king has been hung." Since every person is in God's image, God is disgraced when even a criminal is disgraced.[114]

The rabbis say that slapping the cheek of a fellow Jew is as if slapping the cheek of the *Shechinah*![115] We can expand the reference to all human beings and say that one should never cause unjust harm to another person! The powerful imagery of slapping the *Shechinah's* "cheek" and hanging the *Shechinah*, whose "head and arms" are pained, suggests the most intense and intimate "bodily" involvement of the *Shechinah* in human suffering. When we deal with other humans we are dealing with God Himself.

A holy person experiences other people's suffering as his own suffering. From another perspective: He feels the *Shechinah's* participation in human suffering as his own. When someone once expressed his astonishment at Rabbi Moshe Leib of Sassov's ability to share other people's suffering, the Rebbe said, "What do you mean 'share'? It's my own suffering; how can I not suffer it?"[116] Rabbi Hershele of Nadvorna said that he learned from his master the Baal Shem Tov that when you see someone suffering, you must help him immediately (as in the previously quoted Baal Shem Tov story, "How Could I Wait?"). He taught: "Whenever you see anyone suffering, no matter who it is— whether someone important or ordinary, wicked or contemptible, a Jew or a non-Jew, even an animal, a bird, or an insect— you must act immediately to ease his pain and relieve his suffering, doing everything you can, even beyond your abilities, to help him. And this is the essence of Judaism."[117]

D'VEKUT OF RATZO AND D'VEKUT OF SHOV

There is an unfortunate tendency for people to emphasize the *mitzvot* that concern the relationship between a person and his Maker over the *mitzvot* that concern the relationship between one person and another. We often prefer Torah study, prayer, and meditation over humane deeds, such as kindness and charity. This tendency is always opposed by the true *tzaddikim* (holy people). A person pursuing a mystic path must also learn to balance these two aspects of religion.

A true religious perspective depends on an awareness of priorities. All of a person's deeds should be *mitzvot*, dedicated to God and performed with God-consciousness; but not all deeds are equal. When a father tells his son to take out the garbage and also to respect his mother, the son is right to judge both as important, because they are commands of his father; but if he equates taking out the garbage with respect for his mother, he makes a grave mistake.

Rabbi Eliezer Papo in *Pele Yo'aitz* speaks of a person's "Father and Mother – the Holy One, blessed be He, and His *Shechinah*."[118] The Holy One, blessed be He, is our Father and the *Shechinah* – the Soul of the world and of humanity – is our Mother. To worship God by loving humanity is primary in Judaism. Just as a man derives more pleasure when someone does good to those whom he dearly loves – his wife or children – than when someone does good to him himself, so God derives more pleasure from an act that benefits humans than from an act by which He Himself is worshiped. Rabbi Shneur Zalman of Liadi said that love of Israel is greater than love of God, because then a person loves what the Beloved loves.[119] According to hasidic teaching, love of Israel precedes love of God in the order of divine service; in other words, by loving people one attains love of God.[120] The Baal Shem Tov said: "Love of Israel is the first gate leading into the courtyards of God."[121]

Two of the main ways to serve God, to achieve *d'vekut* with Him, are by prayer and by service to fellow humans. These are the two main aspects of the Baal Shem Tov's Hasidism, with both cited to explain how he reached his high spiritual levels (see p.26). Hasidic mysticism teaches that there must be complementary spiritual "movements" of *ratzo* and *shov*, respectively, "running" to God– in prayer and other meditative practices– and "returning" to the world– to do God's will here, in acts of kindness for other humans, for example. But this back and forth movement of *ratzo* and *shov*, of running and returning, must be properly understood for, according to the unified mystic perspective, nothing is separate from God. Neither is this world separate from God. There is nothing but God. Rather, there is, so to speak, God separate from and beyond this world and God within this world. In the usual conception people have of "God and the world," what they ordinarily call "God" is only a part or an aspect of God. Jewish mystics call the transcendental God: the Holy One, blessed be He (the root meaning of "holy" is "separate") and they call the immanent God: the *Shechinah*, the indwelling Divine Presence. But the two are actually one. All kabbalistic practice is to cause the "marital" union of the "male" Holy One, blessed be He, with the "female" *Shechinah*. So a mystic "runs" to unite with God, the Holy One, blessed be He, who is beyond this world, but he "returns" to unite with God– God in the world, the *Shechinah*.

People often think that separating from the world and materiality in prayer and meditation is the ultimate union with God. In fact, the opposite is true, for the *d'vekut* involved in prayer and meditation is only the first mystic goal; there is a second that is even greater. The ultimate goal for humans is to live and to act spiritually in this material world that God created and into which He put them. If God intended for the soul to achieve union with Him without involvement with materiality, He needn't have created the world and sent the soul down into the world. The purpose of separating from one's normal affairs, to seek *d'vekut* with God through prayer and meditation, is to attach yourself so strongly to God that you will be able afterward to return to your daily life and remain in an exalted state of *d'vekut*, while acting according to God's will. The essence of divine service is to unite with God in the world, with the divinity in the creation, particularly with humans, who are created in His image, and to love and serve them. Rabbi Menachem Mendel Schneersohn, the late Lubavitcher Rebbe, said: "The purpose of prayer is not ultimately to be separated from the world, in *d'vekut* with divinity, but to infuse this *d'vekut* [of prayer] into one's activities [in the world]."[122] "The ultimate purpose is to delight in doing a favor for another Jew."[123] The Rebbe also wrote: "In the *d'vekut* of *ratzo*, a person is occupied only with himself, but [superior to that] in the *d'vekut* of *shov*, he is concerned with others."[124]

One should seek *d'vekut*, union and communion, with God through *d'vekut* with one's fellow humans. It is easiest to see God's presence in those whom we love and respect, such as a cherished spouse or a holy person or pious people in general. The first Torah usage of the root word behind *d'vekut* occurs in Genesis, where it says that a man shall cleave to his wife[125]. The rabbis also talk of cleaving to *tzaddikim*[126] and to pious comrades[127]. One cleaves to God by cleaving to one's spouse and family, to holy people and pious comrades. This cleaving must ultimately be extended to all Jews and non-Jews too, all those who are created in the divine image.

In Hasidism, prayer is the primary spiritual practice for the *d'vekut* of "running," because it involves an intense face-to-face relationship to God. What then is the essential way that a person should achieve *d'vekut* with God in the way of *shov*, of "returning" to this world and doing God's will? By *d'vekut* with fellow humans, by serving God in humanity, by doing good to other people because they are in God's image. We must develop not only mystic God-consciousness, to be aware of God at all times, but also mystic people-consciousness, to be aware of the essential divinity of all other humans here with us; we should be acutely aware of other people and see them as being in the image of God. As previously said, the

Baal Shem Tov attained his spiritual levels by his fervent praying and by his devoted love of the children for whom he was caring when he was an assistant teacher.

The Besht's Baby Grasps His Father's Beard

The following tale teaches a lesson about the relation between "running" to God in meditation and "returning" to God in this world by compassionate concern for people.

When the Besht was still a young man engaged in the intensive spiritual practices that raised him to the exalted spiritual levels he attained, he and his wife Hannah rented an inn near a small village. The Besht built for himself a secluded hut in the forest and he prayed, studied Torah, and meditated there day and night, the whole week.

His wife ran the inn, and God blessed the work of her hands and she was successful. They received guests for lodging and meals. When guests arrived, she sent for the Baal Shem Tov and he came and served them. If there were no guests, the Besht remained in solitude in the forest throughout the week, fasting from Sabbath to Sabbath, and on Friday he came home to the inn. On the Sabbath evening, he sat at the table in a mystic trance of such awesome *d'vekut* that he did not eat. His holy wife, anxious for him to eat after his fast, called to him, so that he would return to body consciousness, but she was not able to draw his mind down to this world.

Once, she put their infant son Tzvi on his father's lap, as the Baal Shem Tov sat at the table, and the child began to pull at his father's holy beard, as children do. This drew the Besht's mind back to this world and he began to eat. From then on, the Besht's wife always placed the child on his father's lap at the table on Friday night, to draw his mind down, so that he would eat, for although the Besht's thoughts might be roaming in the highest heavens, he was immediately drawn down to body consciousness to attend to a child.[128]

Rabbi Shneur Zalman's Lesson to His Son about a Baby

A story about Rabbi Shneur Zalman of Liadi, the first Lubavitcher Rebbe, and Dov Ber, his son, who succeeded him as Rebbe, clarifies the point of the previous tale:

> Rabbi Dov Ber was living in his father's house after his marriage. Once he was sitting and studying Torah in the same room in which an infant was sleeping. Suddenly, the infant rolled out of its crib, fell to the floor, and began crying loudly. Rabbi Dov Ber, who was totally immersed in his Torah study– in a trance of *d'vekut*, with his mind and senses concentrated on the subject of his study– did not even hear the baby crying and continued studying.
>
> Rabbi Shneur Zalman was at that time sitting in his room, down the hall, some distance from where the child was crying, and of course there were walls separating the rooms. He also was in a trance studying Torah, yet he immediately heard the baby's cries. He went into the room where the infant was wailing, put him back in his crib, and quieted him down; then the rabbi returned to his room and his study. Later, he reproached his son saying, "It's true that a person should be totally immersed in his study; nevertheless, one must hear a baby crying and care for him."[129]

When Rabbi Menachem Mendel Schneersohn, the late Lubavitcher Rebbe, told this story he noted that even though a person is involved in mystic meditations he must interrupt them and attend to a baby, who is a part of God.

Rabbi Shneur Zalman Leaves His Praying to Help a Woman

In the preceding tale, Rabbi Shneur Zalman, who was in a

state of *d'vekut* while studying Torah, pulled himself away to help a baby. Another story about Rabbi Shneur Zalman tells:

> Once, while he was praying on Yom Kippur in Liozni and– as goes without saying for someone of his spiritual level– was in a state of intense *d'vekut*, he heard that a woman who had recently delivered a child had been left alone and unattended in bed, while everyone else had gone to the synagogue. The Rebbe took off his tallis and went to the outskirts of the town, to the woman, to prepare food and drink for her and serve her (a new mother is exempt from fasting on Yom Kippur).[130]

The Tzemah Tzedek, the third Lubavitcher Rebbe, grandson of Rabbi Shneur Zalman and son of Rabbi Dov Ber, said: "All the self-sacrifice [in divine service] of my grandfather, the first rebbe, was as nothing compared to his self-sacrifice when he had to separate himself from "and on earth I desire no one beside You" (Psalm 73:25) and devotedly do a favor for a Jew."[131] While praying or studying Torah the Rebbe had no thought or interest in anyone or anything but God– and who can imagine the yearning with which he cleaved to God when praying (on Yom Kippur!) or when studying Torah?– yet he pulled himself away to cleave to Him by helping a person created in His image. But if the whole purpose of creation is for a person to act in this world, why should it require such self-sacrifice for the Rebbe to pull himself away from his ecstatic closeness to God in praying or studying? Because, said the late Lubavitcher Rebbe, only when a person yearns for the intensity of a direct and unmediated attachment to God is he able to maintain his *d'vekut* while engaged in this-worldly activity, such as serving fellow humans.[132]

mportant than Ecstasy

The previous Lubavitcher Rebbe, Rabbi Joseph Isaac Schneersohn, told this story:

During the winter of 1913, when I was 33 years old, I went to visit my holy father [who was then Lubavitcher Rebbe, Rabbi Sholom Dov Ber] in Menton, France. Menton is a seaside resort town. Every day he and I would walk together for hours along the seashore and talk. My father told me many awesome teachings and stories during these walks. He talked especially about meditating on hasidic concepts to prepare for prayer, while wearing tallis and *tefillin*. One day he was telling me about the awesome spiritual effect this kind of meditation has, describing it in numerous ways, saying, for example, that it causes light to come down from the higher realms to illumine the world and a person's soul. "This is true," he said, "of an ordinary person; how much more so of a *tzaddik*, for when a *tzaddik* meditates this way, he experiences a divine bliss and delight and tastes the sweetness of God."

With God's help [said Rabbi Joseph Isaac], I hope to always remember that glorious moment – the sight of my holy father's face flaring in ecstasy as he uttered the words, "the sweetness of God." At that moment, I felt I understood the words of my holy ancestor, Rabbi Shneur Zalman [of Liadi, the first Lubavitcher Rebbe], who defined a *tzaddik* who attains the level of being a *merkavah*, a chariot of God, as someone who never ceases, all his life, even for an instant, from God-consciousness. Seeing my holy father stroll along the splendorous seashore, yet immersed in Godly delight and sweetness, I thought that he was certainly an *atzmi*, a person who lives in God's presence every moment, a person of utmost spiritual integrity, who reveals the essence of his soul and acts identically regardless of who he is talking to or where he is, even in the most beautiful natural surroundings conceivable, as now.

For a long time after my father had spoken about the

bliss and ecstasy of divine meditation before prayer, we walked together silently. I saw that everyone who passed us in the opposite direction stared at my father's face, because it was shining with a holy light. [His father was in a deep trance of *d'vekut*, in an ecstasy of God-con-sciousness.] Suddenly, as if he were waking up from sleep, my father turned to me and said, "Joseph Isaac! I want you to know that the ecstasy a person gains from meditating before prayer, whether he is an ordinary person or even a *tzaddik*, is absolutely insignificant compared to what he gains if the Holy One, blessed be He, grants him one thing only: that he have a desire, an inclination, to do a favor for another Jew, that another person be dearer to him than his own self. I tell you, it is worthwhile to toil five hours a day, for five days, toil of the body and toil of the spirit, to comprehend the divine, if the result is that one truly desires to do a Jew a favor!"[133]

For someone else to be dearer to you than your own self, as in the Rebbe's words, you must identify primarily with your divine soul and your larger Self, the *Shechinah*, rather than with your body. When you realize that another person is in God's image, you will love him not only "as your (small) self" but even more than your self.[134]

D'VEKUT WITH ALL OF CREATION BUT ESPECIALLY WITH PEOPLE

All creation is one and filled with divinity. God's glory fills the world and there is no place where He is not present. The goal of a Jewish mystic is to identify totally with the divine unity and to experience herself as part of the unity.

In the Book of Genesis story about the Garden of Eden (the ideal world), the Torah says that humans should "tend" the Garden: We are the caretakers whom God has made responsible for the planet as a whole and for all of its animal and plant life. If we serve God by caring for His creation, God directs the creation to serve us. The Torah says that God made all the animals pass before Adam, for him to give them names, but no partner was found for him. Then God created the woman to be his partner. The Torah continues by saying that a man *cleaves* to his wife (using a word from the same Hebrew root as *d'vekut*).[135] The first appearance of a word in the Torah is the "headquarters" for understanding its meaning.[136] One meaning derived from the reference to *d'vekut* here is that although we must serve the world from a sense of identity with all creatures and creations, and perceive its divine oneness, a person can only truly cleave to other human beings.

The Divine Presence pervades God's creation, but there are greater and lesser manifestions of divinity. Living creatures – such as animals and plants – manifest His Being more than ordinary inanimate objects, for He is a living God. Humans manifest His divinity even more, for they are created in His image with a potential for holiness and goodness. Torah scholars and pious people manifest Godliness still more because they strive to preserve the divine image. Holy people most powerfully manifest divinity, because they imitate God's love and clearly reveal the divine image in which they were created. One aspect of the special greatness of a holy person is that she sees the image of God in all people, even those who are sinful and wicked, in whom it is covered up and hidden, and she loves them and seeks their good. A holy person also shows reverence for all of the creation, for animals, plants, and even inanimate things.

To achieve *d'vekut* with God in His creation, a Jew must focus first on cleaving to holy people, scholars, and the pious, then on cleaving to all fellow Jews and to all humans created in God's image. Finally, a Jew should see Godliness everywhere. According to hasidic teaching, the Baal Shem Tov's path is: Everything is divinity; divinity is everything.[137] Therefore, like Adam in the Garden of Eden, we should serve God by caring for and serving His creation. We should relate to all God's creatures and creations with love and respect, with the mystic awareness that all existence is infused with His Presence. But our primary focus must always be on seeing the divinity in our fellow humans and on loving and serving God in humanity.

UNDERSTANDING THE *D'VEKUT* OF IMITATING GOD'S LOVE

The ancient rabbis taught that we can cleave to God in *d'vekut* by imitating His nature and attributes, by being loving, giving, patient, and forgiving. They said: "Be like Him: As He is merciful, so should you be merciful; as He is giving, so should you be giving [and so on for the other attributes]." Rabbi Noson Tzvi Finkel, the Slobodker Rabbi, explained that only by acting *like* God, does a person fully reveal in himself God's *likeness* and image. According to the Slobodker, the divine attributes of mercy are rooted in our divine image; by imitating and manifesting those attributes, we reveal our Godly image.[138] Rabbi Noson Tzvi taught:

> The Holy One, blessed be He, called Jacob "god," as it says, "and He, the God of Israel, called him [Jacob] 'god'"[139]. All Jews merit this title, because of their free will, which allows them to *imitate God's attributes, for only in that way can they reflect the image of God and reveal His likeness*, so to speak. And this is true not only of Jews, but of all human beings, because every human created in the divine image and having the power of free will is worthy of reaching this greatness.[140] (Italics added)

Rabbi Shalom Noah, the Slonimer Rebbe, writes that all the *mitzvot* and all a person's deeds should be directed to achieving *d'vekut* with God; but the ancient rabbis singled out imitating God's loving attributes as specially important in cleaving to God because a person's "attributes," his character traits, are the *source* of his deeds.[141]

The Slonimer Rebbe further teaches that the source of bad character traits, such as anger, jealousy, and pride, is egotism. An egotistical person excessively loves himself and has no love to spare for God or for other people. He can be cured by nullifying himself before God. Only then can he change his bad attributes and repair his attribute of love so that he will be able to love God and other people. The Slonimer Rebbe cites the Baal Shem Tov's teaching on the verse: "I stand between God and you"[142]– your "I" stands as a barrier between you and your Father in Heaven. Therefore, says the Rebbe, the key to cleaving to God is to remove your egotism, to nullify yourself to God and become infused with His "I," and His loving attributes.[143]

We can transform ourselves outwardly by fulfilling God's commandments and inwardly by following God's example and imitating His divine attributes. The mystic path is actions, attributes, and essence. We begin by doing divinely commanded actions, then by imitating and absorbing the divine attributes, until finally we reveal our divine essence, our soul, and become like God.

Perspectives for Understanding

A person cleaves to God in prayer by directing all his love and all his thoughts to God. He cleaves to God by loving and helping– cleaving to– another human in God's image. But how can we understand the mystic cleaving to God by imitating His attributes? Since this is more difficult to grasp, viewing it from different perspectives may help us to comprehend it.

Imagine a disciple winning his spiritual master's favor and getting close to him by obeying his master's instructions regarding his deeds. This is equivalent to obeying God's commandments. But another way for him to get close to his master is by carefully observing his master's personal attributes – his compassion, his patience, and so on– and by thinking about these qualities all the time and imitating them; this is the master's deeper side. This is equivalent to imitating God's merciful attributes. When a spiritual master sees that his disciple is imitating and acquiring his, the master's, purified character traits, that arouses the master's love and affection, and he feels closer to the disciple. *D'vekut* with God is not only from one side: A religious person must do everything to cleave to God, but he succeeds when he arouses God's love and God cleaves to him.

We arouse God's love and favor by doing His will. Therefore, fulfilling the commandments (*mitzvot*) leads to *d'vekut*. But by doing the *essence* of His will and by being like Him – by being loving, giving, patient, and forgiving– we attract His love in the strongest way. Thus, Moses said to God, "Make known to me Your ways, that I may know You, and [then imitate Your ways] so that I may find favor in Your sight"[144].

The Slonimer Rebbe, Rabbi Shalom Noah, relates a short version of a parable taught by a predecessor, Rabbi Abraham of Slonim. The parable explains the relation between a person's character traits and his ability to cleave to God and perceive His presence.

> A king knew that if his son, the prince, always remained near him he would never develop his character, so he sent him away from the palace to a distant province in the kingdom, where the customs were rustic and boorish. Once there, the prince lived and behaved like everyone else in that place, but after a while realized that his character traits and behavior were very bad and he considered that before too long he would have to return to the king's presence. So he imagined that he was standing before the king and the wonderful pleasure he

had from that and thus he was able to uproot his bad character traits. And the more he purified his character traits, the easier he found it to imagine that he was in the king's presence.[145]

This parable teaches that when a person purifies his character by imitating God's attributes, he finds it easier to be aware of God's presence. Therefore, the tradition says that before praying, a person should utter his resolve to love his neighbor as himself. Opening our heart to love people also opens our heart to God. Love for other people expands us beyond the narrowness of our limited self, making us more able to love God and to receive His love.

Another way to understand how, by imitating God's merciful attributes, we cleave to Him, is that by imitating God's loving attributes, we become like Him. Then, since "like attracts like," the love from both sides grows stronger and it is easier to cleave together in *d'vekut*.

Another way to understand the secret of this cleaving: By opening our heart to love people, we become a *channel* for God's attributes; by becoming patient, we become a channel for His patience and so on. Whereas in praying we cleave to God by our love flowing to Him and by opening ourselves to a return flow of His love, in imitating His merciful attributes, we cleave to God by His love flowing *through* us. This latter *d'vekut* becomes even more powerful when we reflect and meditate on our love for others as being God's love, coming from the spark of God in our divine soul.

The Elder of Slobodka offers the following insight and perspective on cleaving to God by imitating His attributes: The essence of our understanding of God is through the way He acts in the world, through His attributes, that He is loving, giving, and so on. Now, the only way to truly understand an attribute is by manifesting it: One understands love by being loving; one understands patience by being patient. Therefore, the key to understanding and knowing God is by imitating

His attributes.[146] The prophet Jeremiah praised one of the Judean kings, saying: "He defended the rights of the poor and the needy, and it was well. Is this not to know Me?"[147] This kind of intimate knowing is a form of cleaving.

Another way to understand cleaving to God by imitating His attributes: According to mystic teaching, the higher levels of our souls are not even within our body, but hover above us, so to speak (the halo); they are merged in God and in constant contact with Him. The soul is a part of God and its higher levels are always in *d'vekut* with Him. However, our ego forms a barrier to our awareness of this reality. When we overcome our egotism and reveal the essence of our divine soul by imitating God's attributes and loving others, the divine soul that is directly connected with God shines through, we realize we are a part of God, we experience our *d'vekut* with God and are infused with His light. Thus, since we are actually a part of God, the *d'vekut* and awareness of God that we attain is not like the love of another but is like the love a person has for himself. Rabbi Moshe of Kossov writes:

> What does it mean to love the Creator, whose presence we can not usually feel or grasp? What do the rabbis mean by their teaching about the commandment "to cleave to Him," [when they say]... "Cleave to His [thirteen merciful] attributes; as He is merciful, so should you be merciful"? If a person examines and transforms all his attributes in order to cleave to God, he will become perfect, and *he will feel within him a natural urge to love the Creator* who teaches him for his good, *just as he has a natural love in his heart for himself,* even though he knows his faults, because it is part of his nature and is within his innards, so will it [*d'vekut* and love for God] be part of his nature if he acts according to God's attributes. About this is it written: "you shall love the Lord your God with all your heart, with all your soul, and with all your might," *because this love is not the love of desire [of something outside one] but a natural love [of Self.* You can

love God so totally because God is within your heart and soul]. (Italics added)[148]

MYSTIC MOTIVES IN LOVING AND SERVING FELLOW HUMANS

From a mystic perspective, what should our attitude and motives be when loving and helping other people?

The great Musar teacher, Rabbi Simha Zissel Ziv, the Kelmer Maggid, explained that even doing good to others as a *mitzvah* is not the highest motive. One should not do acts of goodness and compassion from calculated motives of doing a *mitzvah*, but from a natural affection that is accompanied by generosity and joy.

According to this view, he interpreted "you shall love your neighbor as yourself": "The Torah tells us to seek the other person's good ... [and] to love him, not because it is a *mitzvah*, which would not be real love ... but to love him *as you love yourself*. No one loves himself because "one should love people because God created them," but naturally, without calculations and without limit, and without any ulterior aim. No one would ever say: "I've fulfilled the *mitzvah* of loving myself"; therefore, in the same way, you should love the other person naturally, from joy and pleasure without limit, and without ulterior intentions and justifications.[149]

Mystic love and service of fellow humans flow from a perception of oneness and identity with them. When a person serves other people from a sense of identity, he does so without reflection or calculation. There is no delay; he acts naturally, just as he does not delay when acting on his own behalf. His good deeds for others will not be motivated by mere compassion, just as a person does not act on his own behalf because of compassion. But it is only by cultivating our compassion and opening our heart more and more that we will eventually, with God's help, achieve the higher perception of our identity with all humanity.

Together with an increasing awareness of our inner identity with other people, we should realize that by loving and serving them we are actually loving and serving God Himself, that the person before us represents the Shechinah, that he or she is an actual divine image. When this perspective becomes real in our lives, we will relate to people with reverence as well as love; when we help them, we will not condescend, from above to below, but serve them from below to above, because our intention when we help them should be that we are serving God in them.

Therefore, sympathy and pity are not in themselves adequate motives for serving others. A frequent problem when giving charity and helping others is that the receiver can easily be made to feel inferior and he resents the giver. If a person serves others with a recognition that he is serving God, he will not pity or condescend, but will serve them with reverence and humility. Rabbi Elimelech of Lizensk wrote: "There are people who are concerned about their fellows' troubles because of their soft heart and their pity, and that is also good, but it is not the true way. The true way is when a person feels the suffering of another Jew because this is the suffering of the Shechinah, as it is written: 'I am with them in all their troubles'[150] and his only goal is to draw good to Israel in order to lift up the Shechinah."[151]

The true motives for love and service to fellow humans are like those of a nurse serving her ill queen— love and compassion for an ill person mixed with reverence and humility for her queen. When one helps or serves another person with this spiritual awareness, the dignity of the person helped is not lowered, but elevated.

No human being can help or harm another person if God does not decree it. We must realize that we can not help anyone else but can only be His agents to benefit someone; and He has many other agents to do His will if we do not.[152] Since God alone determines the fate and welfare of all creatures, it is even arrogant to imagine that, without Him, we can do good to another human. The Slobdodker taught: "The essence of a kind deed is not the deed itself but its spiritual aspect, because if Providence decrees that this happen, it will happen one way or the other, even if this particular person does not do the deed, for God does not need human assistance. What does God ask from a person? That he act with a single-minded focus and intention that will reveal the inner source of his deed, which is the divine attribute rooted in his divine image, and thereby reveal his divine image."[153]

Therefore, the essential motive in loving our neighbor, when we seek to do good and to help someone, is to realize that we cannot really help anyone and to intend by our actions, first and foremost, to *serve God*.

MYSTICISM AND LOVE

We should not think that the mystic path of love is above and beyond us, for in truth, whatever spiritual level we are on, the love we already feel for others stems from the reality of our mystic connection with them. All people, on the soul-level, are connected and at one. A mystic who reveals her soul's essence becomes aware of her identity with the souls of others and feels universal love. It is egotism that produces the false feeling of separation between ourselves and others; egotism makes us selfish and unfriendly, even hostile to those who threaten our narrow interests or desires. But by expanding beyond our small, limited self we can realize our identity with other people and open up to love.

Individuals on different spiritual levels love a larger or

smaller circle of people. Even narrow individuals, who love only their immediate family, have a dim perception of their oneness with those few people; and they too will usually have at least some sympathy for others beyond their family. When a person loves only a few others, it is because he or she cannot attain more and, in a sense, we can say that she is a mystic or *tzaddeket* within that small circle! Thus, mystic experience is behind all manifestations of love; mysticism and love are intimately connected. Although most people have only an imperfect and limited awareness of mystic reality, their souls know the truth, that we are actually one with all other souls.

All love is, then, "mystic." And the fullness of mystic love already exists hidden within every person's soul; it does not have to be created but only aroused and revealed.[154] Therefore, even non-mystics can start wherever they are spiritually; they can uncover the love hidden within them and steadily expand the circle of their love, for the joy of life comes only from love.

Mystic awareness and open-heartedness should be cultivated together. The Jewish mystic path is for the head and the heart. A Jewish mystic has an expanded consciousness, that is, she is established in a constant state of God-consciousness, but she also has an open heart that flows with love for God and God's creation. We must experience the divine unity of the universe, of all reality, not only in our mind but in our heart, a heart that embraces all of God's creation, with love for all God's creatures, especially human beings.

PRACTICAL LESSONS

How can we fulfill the teachings of mystic humanism— to see others as images of God, as manifestations of the Shechinah, to imitate God's loving attributes and to experience loving and serving our fellow humans as loving and serving God? Our goal must be to not merely enjoy these concepts intellectually but to make them real so that the perspective of mystic humanism affects our behavior and becomes part of our daily life. We previously said that Rabbi Noson Tzvi Finkel of Slobodka worked on himself until his humanistic beliefs were so firmly established within him that they were reflected in all his actions.

LEARNING TO SEE THE DIVINE IMAGE

A parable can help us understand what is required of us:

A king, who was greatly beloved, once traveled to a distant country on matters of state. His people missed him sorely. They were used to being encouraged or consoled by his benevolent presence; even viewing his radiant face inspired them. One day someone had an idea: Many artists had made portraits of their beloved king, each one portraying him according to his own perspective, talent, and skill. So this man said, "Let us put all these portraits in a little museum and whenever we feel longing for our beloved king, we can go to that room, walk through it and see all the portraits. It will be as if we were gazing on the face of the king himself."

These "portraits" of the King are us – all humanity. Each human represents an image of the King according to a particular perspective. That is what the Torah means when it says that humans are made in the "image" of God. And that is the way we should view other people – with mystic vision – as actual "portraits" of God Himself. We must be as radical as the teaching of Genesis that every human is a part or image of God. We might even consider the synagogue a special "museum" in which to cultivate love for our fellow Jews by viewing them as images of God.[155]

Rabbi Shlomo Carlebach (the memory of a tzaddik for a blessing) quoted the Baal Shem Tov as saying that when you meet somebody, you should say to yourself: "I'm going to fulfill the commandment to love your neighbor, with this person before me."[156] Giving this teaching a mystical turn can mean that, when you look at someone, you say to yourself, as a brief meditation: "This person is an actual image of God!" and resolve to act accordingly. Consider, for example, how she would appear if she actually fulfilled her potential to manifest the divine image and was a radiant holy person. And, after all, what do we know of a person's inner life? How can we know the holiness of a person? Do other people appreciate the holiness and preciousness of those whom you know intimately and love? So, reflect on the inner light of each person's soul, even though it may be obscured, and treat all people according to who they might be and who they are in essence, rather than according to their limitations, faults, and failings. An early hasidic book suggests momentarily meditating on a person as manifesting the Shechinah: "When you see any person, imagine the Being of God and His effulgent light flooding through him to you."[157]

One way to increase our ability to see others as holy and as images of God is to begin where it is easiest: by developing and cultivating our appreciation of those whom we already consider to be holy people, to focus on the way they reflect

God's image and light, until we clearly see their holiness. A holy person is someone whom we cannot look at without being reminded of God, whose presence hovers around her. But one reason a holy person is holy is that she considers all other people holy and cannot look at *anybody* without being reminded of God; that is the level we must strive to reach by persistent practice.

Special times to concentrate on a mystic vision of other people are when helping or doing good to them or when receiving help from them. When a family member, friend, or someone else shows us kindness, we should realize that he or she is manifesting God's love for us and see her as an image of God.

LEARNING TO IMITATE GOD'S LOVE

A person naturally becomes like someone he thinks about all the time. Therefore, one may become like God by continually meditating on Him and on His loving attributes. We should model our behavior on God's ways, studying about His attributes to understand them fully and thinking about them constantly to know when to apply them. A person can achieve this by studying books[158] about the Thirteen Attributes, such as Rabbi Moshe Cordovero's *Palm Tree of Deborah*. He can reflect and meditate on the divine attributes, to absorb the lessons they teach for his behavior. Rabbi Cordovero suggests that a person continually meditate on the Thirteen Attributes and keep the Torah verse[159] about them in his mouth always as a memorial – in other words, use it as a mantra. Then, when the situation arises, he will remember, and say, "Now, I should be compassionate" or "giving" or "patient." And he should resolve in advance that at such times, he will, without fail, act as he should.

FAMILY

One prime area of our lives in which we may cultivate a mystic view of our fellow human beings, is the family. The Torah says that spouses "cleave" to each other in marriage and the two become one flesh. Because of the bond formed between husband and wife, it is easier for them, if they merit it, to see that the *Shechinah* is between them and to realize their mystic oneness. The Talmud says that when Rabbi Joseph heard the footsteps of his mother approaching, he would rise quickly, and say, "The *Shechinah* is coming!"[160] If we see our family members as images of God, as manifestations of the *Shechinah*, our devotion to them will become infused with reverence. The Maggid of Mezritch said that God has given us our loved ones, who are always with us in our home, so that we will always be reminded of Him.[161] If a mother spends much of her time caring for her child, she can make the child a focus for her mystic meditation by considering it as an image of God. There is a special manifestation of Godliness in parents (as in the anecdote about Rabbi Joseph) and also in children.

Rabbi Simha Bunim of Pshis'cha told his disciple, Rabbi Samuel of Shinova, that whenever Rabbi Samuel did anything for him, he should intend it as a *mitzvah*, a divine commandment.[162] Serving one's spiritual master has a special significance in terms of serving God, but the principle applies as well to serving family and friends. We should consider everything we do for loved ones as a *mitzvah*. We can further give our kindness a mystic meaning by striving, while doing kind acts for family members, to see our identity with them. From that higher perspective, we should love them as we love ourself – not as a *mitzvah* but naturally, from self-love. Then, as we increase in love and as our heart opens, we can spread our love more and more to those outside our circle of family and friends.

WORK

Another area of our lives that can be infused with mystic spirituality and loving service for others is in our work for a livelihood. According to hasidic teaching, every person, in her innermost heart, which even she herself often does not know, wants to be kind and do good to her fellow humans. Everyone who works – as a doctor, teacher, or businessperson – serving others' needs for money, is, in her heart, working for the sake of doing good; the money she receives for her trouble is secondary and unimportant, because she obviously has to accept money in order to live. Therefore, everyone who works to serve others is fulfilling the *mitzvah* of kindness.[163]

Mystically speaking, the reason everyone inwardly yearns to be kind is that on the soul level everyone knows, even without knowing it consciously, that she is connected and at one with all other humans. The goal is to bring these truths into our consciousness – by reminding ourself of them as we work – so that they open our heart. A teacher, for example, can occasionally utter prayers such as: "God, by teaching these children I hope to love and serve them and You, because they are made in Your image!" A businessperson can say: "God, let me perceive my oneness with all people because I know that on the soul level, we are all one. Let my motive at work be to make money to support myself and my family but also to help the people whom I'm serving. I know that by helping them I am serving You because they are manifestations of the *Shechinah!*"

GOOD DEEDS AND VOLUNTEER WORK

We can also follow the mystic path of loving people in our good deeds and our volunteer work. Many of the Torah's commandments are about giving charity, clothing the naked, visiting the sick, and comforting mourners. When we do these good deeds, we should be aware of their larger spiritual meaning in fulfilling the Torah's essence, which is to love our neighbor as ourself, to imitate God's merciful attributes, and ultimately, to realize our mystical identity with all human beings and achieve *d'vekut* with the *Shechinah*.

One can worship God when praying in the synagogue and one can also worship Him when doing volunteer work in the hospital or in the shelter for the homeless. If we do good deeds as a spiritual practice— as a way to elevate ourselves spiritually and draw closer to God and to people— we will have a different attitude about what we are doing. If a person serves fellow humans as *part of a mystic path*, from mystic motives, considering his or her work as a service of God, she will then be as attentive to the means involved in her work as to the ends. The work will be as spiritually important to the helper as to the one helped. The Elder of Slobodka taught that the purpose of a kind deed is not only to fulfill the need of the recipient, but to spiritually elevate the person doing the kindness.[164]

Fixing the Bed

The following hasidic tale illustrates this point.

> One winter night, when the whole town of Nadvorna was asleep and Rabbi Mordechai, the Rebbe of Nadvorna, was occupied in his holy service of Torah study and prayer, the Rebbe heard some knocking on his window. He went to look to see who it was and saw that it was an elderly Jew who had just arrived in town.
> The Rebbe let him in and welcomed him, offering him hospitality. Since the man was cold, hungry, and tired, the Rebbe immediately stoked the oven to warm

him, ran to bring him something to eat and drink, and
then ran to get pillows, sheets, and a blanket to fix a bed
for him. The man, who did not know that this was the
Rebbe, was anyway upset that his host was going to such
bother for him. "Please," he said, "don't trouble yourself
so much for me. I can fix the bed for myself." The Rebbe
smiled at him and said, "My dear friend, please understand, I'm not fixing the bed for you; I'm fixing the bed
for myself."[165]

The Rebbe meant that by fixing the man's physical bed he
was also fixing his own spiritual bed. Proverbs 11:17 says: "A
kind person is being kind to his own soul."

The essence of kindness as a spiritual practice is for a person
to act with self-sacrifice, disregarding his smaller self to think
of the welfare of others, and giving wholeheartedly with no
thought of return. The more a person thinks of others' welfare,
the more selfless he will become. The boundaries of his self
will expand until he sees others as within his self. When a
person deeply loves a family member – a spouse or child –
that is what happens. The spiritual goal is to achieve this
awareness in relation to others beyond the family, to identify
with our divine soul and to expand and merge our identity
with the community of souls and with our larger Self, the
Shechinah.

Kind deeds should be done with spiritual awareness. A
hospital volunteer should care for the sick not only compe-
tently but with love and reverence for them and for God. He
should work with a devotional attitude, thinking of God and
the religious meaning of what he is doing. He should have
kavvanah, a focused holy intent – just as he would when praying. And just as the spiritual value of a person's praying
depends on his inner devotion to God, on his kavvanah, so
does the spiritual value of his kindness to fellow humans
depend on his kavvanah. If he intends when serving people
to serve God, his deeds will bring him close both to people

and to God.

The traditional rule for applying the commandment to love your neighbor as yourself is the Golden Rule – to treat others "as yourself," as you would want to be treated. Understood mystically, this means to realize that others are part of your own self. This is a high spiritual level but we should not think we can never attain it. We should try to move forward step by step. Rabbi Eliezer Papo teaches in *Pele Yo'aitz*:

> A person should act with kindness whenever possible, with his body, money, and words for, whether the kind deed is great or small, he is doing a *mitzvah*. He should accustom himself to be kind [by beginning with small deeds of kindness]– to open the door for someone knocking, to make change for someone who needs a bill changed, to hand something to a person who needs it. ... All these kind deeds fulfill [and will train you to eventually completely fulfill] "you shall love your neighbor as yourself." [Follow the Golden Rule:] Always imagine how you would want to be treated, and treat others that way.[166]

Just as a spiritually serious person makes Torah study and prayer a regular part of his religious life and of his daily schedule, so should he make charity, acts of kindness, and favors part of his schedule; and he should act with a mystic intention. The Kelmer Maggid said that you have to train yourself to love people, the first step being to delve into the problem of how to accomplish this and to think of it constantly.[167] Rebbe Samuel of Lubavitch said that every Jew should spend fifteen minutes a day to consider what favor he can do for a fellow Jew.[168] Rabbi Isaiah Horowitz (the Shelah) wrote that a person should not let a day pass without his doing an act of kindness with his body or his money.[169] Rabbi Moshe of Kobrin said: "A day in which a Jew does not do a favor for another Jew does not count as a day of his life."[170] One can have a special time for this each day, as did the

Hafetz Hayim, who said: A person may spend the whole day studying Torah, but if he does not set aside part of his day to do deeds of kindness, what a lack of intelligence![171]

> Rabbi Meir'l of Tiktin tried to do some act of kindness before eating his first meal of the day. He made a rule not to taste any food until he had done some favor. Since God fulfills the will of His servants, an opportunity to do a kindness or favor for someone came to Rabbi Meir'l every day.
>
> But one day no such chance came his way and he fasted the whole day. At night he did not go to sleep but went outside to the street. Behold, there was a wagon full of wooden boards in front of his house. He ran to the house of the carpenter, knocked on his door to wake him up, and brought him back with him. The carpenter asked the peasant who owned the wood its price and found that the price was low and the wood was just what he needed for his work.
>
> But unfortunately, though at that price it was a real buy, he did not have enough money to pay for it. Since one *mitzvah* leads to another, Rabbi Meir'l had a chance to do another *mitzvah*, of loaning the carpenter the money. He gladly did so, and then went into his house to eat his first meal of the day, full of joy.[172]

STRIVING TO ACHIEVE

It requires an intense effort to see the *Shechinah* in people and to imitate God's love. We should often pray for God's help to succeed. One way to make progress is by frequently examining our behavior and motives: Are our actions imitating divine love? Are we helping someone because it is an opportunity to serve God in the person? In feeding our child or in feeding a poor person, we should think that we are actually feeding an image of God, feeding God, so to speak. In caring for a sick person, we should remind ourselves that we are actually caring for an image of God, caring for God, so to speak. The *Shechinah* suffers when a human is hungry or ill. When we help people who are in need or who are suffering, we should intend to assuage the suffering of the *Shechinah*. While we are helping, we should offer prayers such as: "God, open my heart to others. Let me see my identity with them and let me see You in them. Let me strive to do good to all and to always act from love."

CONCLUSION

The goal of Jewish mysticism is for a person to find God in his or her lifetime, to experience at every moment the beauty, sweetness, and holiness of the Divine Presence. But only by loving people can we truly love God. Only by meeting people in the deepest way can we truly meet God. By loving and helping others selflessly, God reveals Himself in our heart. Therefore, compassion and kindness, together with Torah study, prayer, and meditation, must be our path to the mystic goal.

Each generation must reclaim and renew the Jewish tradition for itself. We must also renew the mystic tradition not just in theory but in practice; we must seek God-experience and realization. We must use the compelling and potent teachings the tradition offers us in order to express our generation's vision, which to many of us means emphasizing love for God and love for people, and merging mysticism with humanism.

Finding that our intuition – about love of people being the essence of Judaism – is deeply rooted in the Torah, inspires us and reinforces our determination to love and to open our heart. We must love our fellow Jews with devotion, fervor, and the greatest commitment, but we must also expand the circle of our love to be more and more inclusive. Why should our Judaism be small, God-forbid? God said to the prophet Isaiah, "It is too light a thing that you should be My servant to raise up the tribes of Jacob and to restore the preserved of

Israel; I will give you as a light to the nations, that My salvation may reach to the end of the earth."[173] To accomplish our divine mission as Jews, we must preach and practice love for all people.

The ideas and ideals contained in this booklet can become real for us if we make them so. The rabbis teach that one way to absorb a particular spiritual perspective is by immersing ourselves in its study – reading and thinking about it continually. To that end, we can reread this booklet often and reflect and meditate on its teachings, until they enter our bones, so that we not merely admire and cherish them but fulfill them in practice.

The principles of mystic humanism may also be applied to Jewish group activity. People involved in synagogue programs of good deeds should be encouraged to deepen their spiritual relation to their volunteer work. If such programs are integrated into a synagogue's spiritual life, they will not seem like mere social work but will increase both the social consciousness and spiritual consciousness of participants. Religious schools, yeshivahs, and rabbinical seminaries should organize programs to move their teaching beyond texts to spiritual goals that fulfill the texts. As part of this, they can direct their students to social service activities that are given a mystic context. A spiritually-oriented humanism can even help to inspire new social movements and programs in the Jewish world.

When we strive to follow God's will and pray for His help, we receive His divine blessing giving us the strength to succeed and to reach the goal of love and happiness that God intends for us and for all people.

My God and God of my father and mother, I have written this booklet for my own edification. I beg You to enable me to fulfill its teachings. May my heart be open to love all people; may I love in the way that You love. May I utterly forget anger and impatience. May I do favors and acts of kindness always. Please help me to make this real in my life, in the merit of all the holy Jewish men and women of this and previous generations. May it be Your will.

Notes

1. Rabbi Moshe Cordovero's *Tomer Devorah* (*The Palm Tree of Deborah*), and a few other kabbalistic books, might seem to be exceptions to this statement, but, although Rabbi Cordovero's ethical and humanistic teaching is certainly important and of great value, even his system of Kabbalah focuses primarily on heavenly not human matters (see p.24). Whereas ethics may be merely one aspect among many in a religious or mystic worldview, humanism implies that loving people is the central focus within the larger focus on God.

2. Leviticus 19:18

3. Leviticus 19:34

4. P.170b. Rabbi Kimhi adds that the great kabbalist, Rabbi Hayim Vital, writes: "One must love all people, including non-Jews" (*Sha'ar HaKedushah*, section 1, gate 5).

5. *No'am Elimelech*, Vayishlah, p.15b

6. H. Lifshitz, *Shivhei HaRaya* (Jerusalem: Machon HaRaya, 1979), p.6, quoting *Arpalei Tohar*, p.22.

7. S. Raz, *Malachim Kivnei Adam* (Jerusalem: Kol Mevasair, 1994), p.264

8. Genesis 2:7

9. Numbers 33:52; 2 Chronicles 23:17; etc.

10. Genesis 18:19

11. Genesis 18:1f.

12. Genesis 18:23f.

13. Genesis 22:1f.

14. Exodus 2:11-18

15. Deuteronomy 6:5

16. Leviticus 19:18

17. Leviticus 19:34

18. Genesis 18:1

19. *Midrash HaGadol* on Genesis 18:3. The *Targum* on 18:22 says that Abraham *continued praying* after the interruption of the three visitors. See also *Midrash Lekah Tov* on 18:1,2 and *Midrash HaGadol* on 18:22.

20. *Midrash HaGadol* on Genesis 18:4

21. *Erubin* 5:1, 22b

22. *Midrash HaGadol* on Exodus 18:12

23. *Shabbat* 31a

24. *Avot d'Rabbi Natan-B*, chap.26

25. *Targum Yonatan ben Uzziel* on Leviticus 19:18

26. See, for example, Rabbi E. Papo, *Pele Yo'aitz* (Brooklyn, N.Y.: Yerushalayim, 1985), p.110 and S. Raz, *A Tzaddik in Our Time* (New York: Feldheim, 1978), p.413.

27. *Genesis Rabba* 24-7 on 5:1; *Sifra*, Kedoshim, 89a; Y. *Nedarim* 9

28. *Avot* 3:18

29. Leviticus 19:18

30. Y. *Nedarim* 9

31. Rabbi Shalom Noah Berzhovsky, *Netivot Shalom* (Jerusalem: Yeshivat Beit Avraham Slonim, 1995), pp.67,76,79, etc., referring to the rabbis' teachings in *Sifre*, Eykev; *Sotah* 14a, etc., on Deuteronomy 11:22, 13:5, etc.

32. Exodus 33:13

33. See, for example, the words of Rabbi Israel Salanter in D. Katz, *Tenuat HaMusar* (Jerusalem: Feldheim, 1996), vol.1, p.43 and of Rabbi Joseph Isaac Schneersohn, the previous Lubavitcher Rebbe, *Likkutei Dibburim* [English](Brooklyn, N.Y: Kehot, 1992), vol.2, pp.123-124.

34. Deuteronomy 6:4,5

35. Leviticus 19:18

36. *Midrash HaGadol*

37. *Sifre* Deuteronomy 49; *Berachot* 7a

38. *Rosh HaShanah* 16b in the name of the School of Hillel.

39. Rabbi Yisrael Kushta, *Mikveh Yisrael* (Livorno, 1851), #59. I intend to publish an essay proving that this tale is an old *midrash*.

40. Versions of this story do not explicitly mention that the brothers are gentile, yet that fact is known from the Torah story that a prophet told King David the site for the altar of the future Temple (2 Samuel 24:1-25 and 1 Chronicles 21:1-22:1).

41. Isaiah 56:7

42. Ed. Rabbi M. Miller, *The Palm Tree of Deborah* (Israel: Feldheim/Targum, 1993), p.xii

43. *The Palm Tree of Deborah*, chap.1, sect.4

44. *The Palm Tree of Deborah*, chap.1, sect.4

45. Ed. N. Leibman, *Butzina d'Nehorah* [teachings of R. Baruch of Medzibuz] (Israel: 1970), on Psalm 107

46. *Tzava'at HaRivash* (Brooklyn, N.Y.: Kehot, 1982), #41

47. the aspect of *"mah"*— "what" or "nothing"— that is, humility in the soul

48. A. H. Glitzenstein, *Sefer HaToldot* (Israel: Kehot, 1986), Rabbi Yisrael Baal Shem Tov, vol.2, p.640 and Rabbi Joseph Isaac Schneersohn, *Chassidic Discourses* (Brooklyn, N.Y.: Kehot, 1986), p.411

49. *Sefer HaToldot*, Rabbi Yisrael Baal Shem Tov, vol.2, p.679, quoting *Sefer HaSihot* (1948), p.179

50. B. Landau, *HaBaal Shem Tov u'Vnei Heichalo* (B'nei Brak: Netzah, 1961), p.22; Z. A. Hilsenrad, *The Baal Shem Tov* (Brooklyn, N.Y.: Kehot, 1978) [pamphlet], p.32

51. That seems a reasonable way to understand the legend in *Shivhei HaBesht* of the Besht protecting the children from a werewolf; other stories show the young Baal Shem Tov confronting a wolf to protect a gentile shepherd boy.

52. *Imrei Pinhas HaShalem* (Israel: Mishor, 1988), p.205, #81 and p.204, #77. See p.47 and note 110.

53. *Sippurei Nehmadim*, p.3a (5), in Ed. H. Y. Malik, *Sippurim Nifla'im* (Jerusalem: 1976).

54. *Tenuat HaMusar*, vol.3, pp.124-125

55. H. A. Zeitchik, *HaMe'orot HaGedolim* (Jerusalem: 1969), p.230, #78-80; see also *Or HaTzafun* (Jerusalem: Mosad Haskel, 1978), I, p.42.

56. This sentence is based on *HaMe'orot HaGedolim*, p.230, #78-80. The rest of this paragraph, as well as the preceding paragraph and the two following this one, are from p.233, #85.

57. *Or HaTzafun*

58. *HaMe'orot HaGedolim*, p.233, #85

59. *HaMe'orot HaGedolim*, p.236, #93

60. Ed. D.N. Weinberger, *HaSaba MiSlobodka* (Brooklyn, N.Y.: 1986), p.35

61. *HaSaba MiSlobodka*, p.35

62. Deuteronomy 30:14

63. *HaSaba MiSlobodka*, p.170

64. Leviticus 19:18

65. Rabbi Menachem Mendel Schneersohn, *Likkutei Sihot* (Brooklyn, N.Y.: Kehot, 1983), vol.4, p.17

66. *Sefer HeArachim* [Lubavitch] (Brooklyn, N.Y.: Kehot, 1970), Ahavat Yisrael, p.618

67. Based on *Likkutei Dibburim*, vol.1, p.215, note.

68. P.198

69. J.I. Schochet, *The Mystical Dimension* (Brooklyn, N.Y.: Kehot, 1990), vol.3, "Chassidic Dimensions," p.52, quoting *Keter Shem Tov* (Kehot edition), Hosafot, par. 141.

70. Leviticus 19:18

71. Deuteronomy 6:5

72. *The Mystical Dimension*, vol.3, "Chassidic Dimensions," p.52, quoting *Tanya*, chap. 2, with references to other sources.

73. *The Mystical Dimension*, vol.3, "Chassidic Dimensions," p.52, quoting *Keter Shem Tov* (Kehot edition), Hosafot, par. 18, with references to other sources. See *Likkutei Sihot*, vol.IV, p.17, n.84; *Sefer HeArachim*, Ahavat Yisrael, p.627, 6:2

74. *Sefer HaToldot*, Rabbi Yisrael Baal Shem Tov, vol.2, p.631; literally, not the "whole, but the "essence."

75. *Keter Shem Tov* (Brooklyn, N.Y.: Kehot, 1978), I, #65

76. *Me'ir Einei Yisrael* (Jerusalem: Mosdot Anshei Ma'amad, 1992), II, p.107

77. *Sefer HeArachim*, Ahavat Yisrael, p.621, 5:2 and notes 56 and 57

78. *Kovetz Sippurim* (Brooklyn, N.Y.: Kehot, 1993), 1960-1961, 1960, p.10, #13

79. *Sefer HeArachim*, Ahavat Yisrael, p.621, 5:2 and note 59

80. Deuteronomy 4:15

81. *Sefer HeArachim*, Ahavat Yisrael, #4, p.619

82. *Mesillat Yesharim*, chap.11

83. Rabbi E.E. Dessler, *Strive for Truth*, trans. Aryeh Carmell (Israel: Feldheim, 1989), vol.1, p.130

84. *Otzar HaMahshavah* (Jerusalem: Machon Me'orot Da'at, 1981), II, p.16

85. *Sefer HeArachim*, Ahavat Yisrael, #3, p.618, quoting *Tanya*, chap. 32.

86. Quoted by Rabbi David Zeller in his *Tree of Life* audio tapes (Sounds True).

87. *Sefer HeArachim*, Ahavat Yisrael, #3, p.618

88. I have conflated two stories from *Shivhei HaRaya*, p.184, which seem to refer to the same event.

89. *Netivot Shalom*, p.102

90. Psalm 91:15

91. *Netivot Shalom*, p.98

92. Ed. Rabbi S.M.M. Gorvachov, *Sefer Baal Shem Tov* (Jerusalem), vol.2, p.106, #3

93. *Me'or Einayim* (Brooklyn, N.Y.: 1987), p.53a (105)

94. *Avot* 4:3

95. *Genesis Rabba* 24-7 on 5:1. Compare *Mechilta*, Yitro, chap. 11.

96. *Yalkut Shimoni* on Leviticus 19:18

97. Exodus 33:19

98. *Midrash HaGadol*

99. *Exodus Rabba* 26 on 17:8

100. *Sefer HeArachim*, Ahavat Yisrael, p.624

101. *Or Torah* (Brooklyn, N.Y.: Kehot, 1979), Hosafot, par. 42

102. Two sources conflated: Rabbi Moshe Nussbaum, *Ahavat Yisrael* (Jerusalem: 1973), p.50 (quoting *Mivaser Tzedek*) and *Shemen HaTov*, 9b, p.18

103. Genesis 33:10; *Tenuat HaMusar*, vol.3, p.125

104. Genesis 33:10; *Tenuat HaMusar*, vol.3, p.125

105. *HaSaba MiSlobodka*, p.76

106. Genesis 33:3

107. Rabbi Natan Netta of Chelm, *Netta Sha'ashu'im* (Jerusalem, 1966), p.25

108. *Avot* 1:12

109. Proverbs 27:19

110. *Imrei Pinhas HaShalem*, p.205, #81 and p.204, #77. It is clear from internal and external evidence that Rabbi Pinhas's teaching reflects the teaching of his master, the Besht.

111. *Kohelet Rabba* on 7:16

112. *Yalkut Shimoni* on Psalm 91:15, #843

113. *Sanhedrin* 46a

114. *Sanhedrin* 46b

115. *Sanhedrin* 58 and Rashi there

116. Ed. and trans. M. Buber, *Tales of the Hasidim* (New York: Schocken Books, 1973), vol.2, p.86, citing *Sefer HaDorot*. This source has only that Rabbi Moshe Leib "always shared in the sufferings of every person as if the suffering was his own." Buber seems to have created this story to dramatize the teaching and it serves that purpose.

117. Ed. P. Shapiro, *Beit Pinhas*, p.80, n.19

118. *Pele Yo'aitz*, p.303

119. *Sefer HeArachim*, Ahavat Yisrael, p.628

120. *Sefer HeArachim*, Ahavat Yisrael, #3, p.629

121. *The Mystic Dimension*, vol.3, "Chassidic Dimensions," p.59, quoting *Keter Shem Tov* (Kehot edition), Hosafot, par.139.

122. *Kovetz Sippurim*, 1960-1961, 1960, p.1

123. *Kovetz Sippurim*, 1960-1961, 1960, p.5

124. *Kovetz Sippurim*, 1960-1961, 1960, p.5

125. Genesis 2:24

126. *Midrash HaGadol* on Deuteronomy 10:20

127. *Avot* 6:5

128. Ed. Y.Y. Kornblit, *Me'ir Einei Yisrael* (Jerusalem: 1991), p.57

129. *Kovetz Sippurim* (Brooklyn, N.Y.: Va'ad Hanochos Hatmimim, 1989), 1954-1955, 1954, p.7

130. *Kovetz Sippurim* 1960-1961, 1960, p.6, #9 and *Kovetz Sippurim* (Brooklyn, N.Y.: Kehot, 1994) , 1971-1974, 1974, p.47, #21.

131. *Kovetz Sippurim* (Brooklyn, N.Y.: Kehot, 1994), 1966-1967, 1967, p.42, #7

132. *Kovetz Sippurim*, 1966-1967, 1967, p.42, #7

133. Ed. and trans. Yanki Tauber, *Once Upon a Chassid* (Brooklyn, N.Y.: Kehot, 1994), p.148

134. *Ahavat Yisrael*, p.34a

135. Genesis 2:24

136. Heard from Rabbi Shlomo Carlebach.

137. *Sefer HaToldot*, Rabbi Yisrael Baal Shem Tov, vol.2, p.631

138. *Tenuat HaMusar*, vol.3, p.121

139. Genesis 33:20; see *Megillah* 18

140. *Or HaTzafun*, II, p.188

141. *Netivot Shalom*, p.98; see also pp.76 and 79.

142. Deuteronomy 5:5. In the context (4:4-5:5), Moses says that the people did not directly *cleave to God* (the "I" in the verse refers to Moses).

143. *Netivot Shalom*, pp.88-89

144. Exodus 33:13

145. *Netivot Shalom*, p.210; the first part of the parable has been shortened to prevent confusion.

146. *Tenuat HaMusar*, vol.3, pp.121-122

147. Jeremiah 22:16

148. *Hegayon Levavi* (Jerusalem: 1970), p.61

149. *Tenuat HaMusar*, vol.2, p.137, quoting a letter of Rabbi Simha Zissel Ziv.

150. Isaiah 63:9 is understood by the rabbis to mean, as here, that God suffers with people.

151. *Ahavat Yisrael*, p.30a, quoting *No'am Elimelech*.

152. See, for example, Mordechai's words to Esther in Esther 4:14.

153. *Tenuat HaMusar*, vol.3, p.122

154. *Sefer HeArachim*, Ahavat Yisrael, p.616, #1, n.14, quoting *Sefer HaSihot*, Siha 400, p.86.

155. See Yitzhak Buxbaum, *Jewish Spiritual Practices* (Northvale, N.J.: Jason Aronson, 1990), p.187.

156. Heard from Rabbi Carlebach.

157. *Or HaGanuz l'Tzaddikim* (Jerusalem: 1966), p.62; see *Jewish Spiritual Practices*, pp.472 and 678.

158. In English: *The Palm Tree of Deborah*; Rabbi A.C. Feuer *Tashlich*: Tashlich and the Thirteen Attributes, (New York: Mesorah, 1983). In Hebrew: Rabbi Y.Y. Hamburger, *Shaarei Rahamim* (Brooklyn, N.Y.: 1988).

159. The tradition states that the Thirteen Attributes that appear in Exodus 34:6,7 also appear in Micah 7:18-20. Rabbi Cordovero uses the latter verse for his exposition.

160. *Kiddushin* 31a,b

161. *Or HaEmet* (B'nei Brak: Yahadut), p.25, quoted in *Jewish Spiritual Practices*, p.33.

162. Y.L. Levine, *Beit Kotzk*: HeArayot She'beHavurah (B'nei Brak: 1972), p.171

163. *Jewish Spiritual Practices*, pp.203-204

164. *Tenuat HaMusar*, vol.3, p.126

165. *Orot Mordechai* (Tzfat: Machon Tzitz HaNezer, 1995), p.291

166. *Pele Yo'aitz*, p.110

167. *Tenuat HaMusar*, vol.2, p.136

168. Rabbi Joseph Isaac Schneersohn, *Sefer HaSihot*, trans. A.H. Glitzenstein (Israel: Kehot, 1992), 1944, p.56, #11

169. Quoted in *Netivot Shalom*, p.99.

170. Quoted in *Netivot Shalom*, p.99.

171. S. Artzi, *Michtivei HaHafetz Hayim HeHadash* (B'nei Brak: Mishor, 1986), vol.2, p.85

172. A.H.S.B. Michelzohn, *Shemen HaTov*, p.111, #125

173. 49:5,6

GLOSSARY

Baal Shem Tov – "The Master of the (Divine) Name"; Rabbi Israel son of Eliezer, the 18th century founder of the modern Hasidic Movement. See **Besht.**

Besht – Acronym for the *Baal Shem Tov.* See **Baal Shem Tov.**

D'vekut – Loving awareness of God; God-consciousness.

High Holidays – **Rosh HaShanah** (the Jewish New Year) and **Yom Kippur** (the Day of Atonement).

Kabbalah – The main branch of Jewish mysticism.

Kavvanah – God-directed intention while performing a religious act.

Kibbutz – Israeli communal settlement.

Lifnim mishurat hadin – Piety beyond the requirements of Jewish religious law.

Maggid – A preacher.

Midrash – Exposition or exegesis of the scriptures, often including parables, sayings, and stories. The *Midrash* is the book or body of teaching, a *midrash* is a particular teaching.

Mitzvah (pl. **Mitzvot**) – A divine commandment.

Musar Movement – A pietistic movement of non-hasidic traditional Jews that began in the 19th century and that emphasizes *musar*– ethics and character development.

Pele Yo'aitz – *Wondrous Advisor*, a book of religious counsels by Rabbi Eliezer Papo.

Ratzo – "Running" to commune with God by meditative religious practices. See **Shov**.

Rebbe – The leader of a hasidic sect.

Rosh Yeshivah – The principal of a yeshivah. See **Yeshivah**.

Sefer HaBrit – *The Book of the Covenant* by Rabbi Joseph Kimhi.

Sha'ar HaKedushah – *The Gate of Holiness* by Rabbi Hayim Vital.

Shechinah – Literally, "the Indwelling"; God as immanent; the Divine Presence.

Shov – "Returning," after meditative spiritual practice, to do God's will in the world. See **Ratzo**.

Tallis – Prayer shawl.

Tefillin – Phylacteries. Two leather boxes containing scriptural verses inscribed on parchment are bound by leather straps onto the arm and head during the weekday morning prayers.

Tzaddeket - A holy woman. See **Tzaddik**.

Tzaddik (fem. **Tzaddeket**; pl. **Tzaddikim**) – A holy man.

Yeshivah – A traditional Jewish religious academy.

Yom Kippur – The yearly Jewish Day of Atonement.

IF YOU ENJOYED THIS BOOKLET AND BENEFITTED FROM IT

☐ Why not send gift copies to friends?

A copy of *An Open Heart* can be purchased for $9.95 + $2.50 (shipping & handling) = $12.45. For each additional copy after the first, add: $9.95 + $1.00 (shipping, etc.) = $10.95. Ten copies cost $80 + $5 (shipping, etc.) = $85. See the order form on p.93. Contact Yitzhak Buxbaum (see p.96) to inquire about discount rates for larger quantities.

☐ Perhaps you might enjoy Volume 1 in The Jewish Spirit Booklet Series:

Real Davvening:
Jewish Prayer as a Spiritual Practice and a Form of Meditation for Beginning and Experienced Davveners

Learn to *davven* (pray) so that it moves you spiritually. Simple traditional meditation techniques can lift your praying immeasurably higher than before, until you actually taste and experience the nearness of God. That is what is called *Real Davvening*.

This booklet will open the gates before you to one of the most important Jewish spiritual practices: *prayer*. It contains practical, easy-to-do teachings that will enliven your *davvening* and your Judaism.

Price: $7.95; shipping & handling costs are the same as for Volume 2 above.

☐ Perhaps you might enjoy Yitzhak Buxbaum's books:

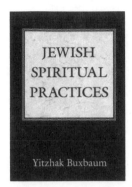

Jewish Spiritual Practices

Softcover, 757 pages
List price: $30.
Discount price: $25 (+ $3 for shipping, etc.)

"Once in a while I read a book that not only makes a profound impression but radically alters my lifestyle. Such a book is *Jewish Spiritual Practices* ..." (*Jerusalem Post*).

"*Jewish Spiritual Practices* is a very, very important book, one which the contemporary Jewish world has been in need of for many years. It is ... the first attempt at a comprehensive guidebook in English to the spiritual dimension of [Jewish religious practices]" (*Wellsprings* [Lubavitch hasidic magazine]).

"*Jewish Spiritual Practices* by Yitzhak Buxbaum ... recently was presented to the Dalai Lama [in India] by an American rabbi who wanted to explain Jewish spirituality to the religious leader." (*Publisher's Weekly*).

The Life and Teachings of Hillel

Hardcover, 376 pages
List price: $35.
Discount price: $30 (+ $3 shipping etc.)

"Buxbaum is a patient and generous religious teacher, writing about Hillel in Hillel's own spirit. This book is filled with learning and profundity, allowing its subject to speak directly to the reader's heart." (Dr. Arthur Green)

Storytelling and Spirituality in Judaism

Softcover, 255 pages
List price: $25.
Discount price: $20 (+ $3 shipping etc.)

The first and only book about sacred storytelling in Judaism and about the hasidic theology of storytelling.

ORDER FORM

To order copies of *An Open Heart, Real Davvening*, or any of Yitzhak Buxbaum's books, send a check payable to Yitzhak Buxbaum, along with this form or a duplicate, to the address on p.96.

Please send the following:

Title	Quantity	Price (incl. shipping, etc.)
An Open Heart		
Real Davvening		
Jewish Spiritual Practices		
The Life and Teachings of Hillel		
Storytelling and Spirituality in Judaism		

*NEW YORK RESIDENTS: *Subtotal*
For shipments sent to a New York address, add
the appropriate sales tax for your area. New York   *Sales tax**
State law requires that tax be paid on the full cost
of the order, including shipping   TOTAL

You are invited to join
The Jewish Spirit Booklet Club

See the statement about the goals of The Jewish Spirit Booklet Series on p.2. Club membership only involves receiving information about publication of new booklets. To join, check the box.

☐ Please enroll me in The Jewish Spirit Booklet Club, to be kept informed about forthcoming booklets.

(Print clearly)

Name

Address

City   State   Zip

Maggid
YITZHAK BUXBAUM

Teacher • Storyteller • Author

YITZHAK BUXBAUM is an inspired and inspiring teacher and storyteller, one of those reviving the honorable calling of the *Maggid* (preacher), who in times past travelled from community to community to awaken Jews to the beauty of their tradition.

Mr. Buxbaum teaches and tells stories with warmth and humor. He often sets the mood by leading singing. And he creates the exciting and enlivening atmosphere of a special event, in which everyone is involved.

Judaism is communicated in a way to reach the committed as well as the curious, those who are near, along with those who are now far – but just need someone to offer them a welcome at the door.

Mr. Buxbaum's approach is not denominational or sectarian and is for Jews of all backgrounds. His programs are appropriate for different age-groups: teens, college-age, adults and seniors.

The programs are entertaining. They are also genuine spiritual experiences. As the Rabbis say: What comes from the heart, enters the heart.

Programs include: LECTURES on topics of Jewish spirituality and mysticism and STORYTELLING of hasidic tales. Inquire about lecture topics.

Mr. Buxbaum leads WORKSHOPS ON DAVVENING that can energize your congregation or havurah. He is available for FULLER SHABBAT PROGRAMS and as a SCHOLAR-IN-RESIDENCE.

Recommendations for
Yitzhak Buxbaum's Teaching and Storytelling

Yitzhak Buxbaum, author of *Jewish Spiritual Practices, The Life and Teachings of Hillel, Storytelling and Spirituality in Judaism, Real Davvening,* and *An Open Heart,* has lectured and told stories at synagogues, JCC's, Y's, Hillels, and retreats, producing enthusiastic responses. He has taught at CAJE conferences, Havurah Movement Summer Institutes, the Elat Chayyim Jewish Retreat Center, the New York Open Center, the New Age Center (Nyack, N.Y.) and the renowned New School for Social Research (New York, N.Y.).

He was honored by being asked to address an audience of rabbis at The New York Board of Rabbis on the topic "The Quest for Spirituality."

"Many thanks for your presentation and for sharing your wonderful insights and delightful teaching manner with all of us." (Rabbi Jeremiah Wohlberg, President, New York Board of Rabbis)

"Yitzhak Buxbaum is a storyteller in the tradition of the great Hasidic masters. He retells their stories with penetrating insight into their relevance for the great and small actions of our lives. People of all backgrounds are powerfully affected by Yitzhak's unique Jewish presence." (Dr. Herb Levine, Hillel advisor, Franklin and Marshall College, Pa.)

"Yitzhak Buxbaum is a gifted spinner of tales. The audience sits enraptured as he unfolds a tale with skill and warmth." (Rabbi William Berkowitz, former head of the Jewish National Fund and Rabbi of Congregation B'nai Jeshurun, New York, N.Y.)

For a brochure and information about programs, contact:

YITZHAK BUXBAUM, Editor
The Jewish Spirit Booklet Series

144-39 Sanford Ave., Apt. 6D-1
Flushing, New York 11355
(718) 539-5978